Praise for
Living in the Family Blender

"I wish you had written this book . . . years ago before my husband and I were married. We might not have struggled as much in parenting our blended family . . . THIS IS AN IMPORTANT BOOK! . . . Your book is so inspiring and should be read by every member of a blended family."

—Barbara J. Scott
Life-educated blended family spouse and parent

Living in the Family Blender

10 Principles of a Successful Blended Family

By

Clark Rich Burbidge and Leah Dee Burbidge

Dedication

To all those who strive to unite; to include; to bring peace and understanding; and most of all, to love unconditionally. We feel certain there is a special place in heaven for those who face the single and blended family gauntlet and never give up. We are honored to walk in your presence.

Everyone is in a blended family.

Courage does not always roar. Sometimes courage is the quiet voice at the end of the day saying, 'I'll try again tomorrow.'

—Mary Anne Radmacher

I have discovered that life is not a series of great heroic acts. Life at its best is a matter of consistent goodness and decency, doing without fanfare that which needed to be done when it needed to be done. I have observed that it is not the geniuses that make the difference in this world…the work of the world is done largely by men and women of ordinary talent who have worked in an extraordinary manner.

—Gordon B. Hinckley

Contents

The Broken Family?

Beginning in 2004 the authors faced a daunting task. Each had five children between the ages of four and twenty-four. Their children faced all the usual challenges associated with growing up. In addition, each future blended family member confronted a world that ignorantly and consistently reminded them they were part of something broken. The reminders usually were not mean-spirited or intentional. However, the term *broken family* hovered like a cloud shadowing every step. Silent unspoken questions, "Does that mean I'm broken too?" and "Is there something wrong with me?" perched on every shoulder.

Bringing this family together became the greatest challenge and opportunity Clark and Leah had ever faced. Fraught with sweat, tears, and a healthy dose of the divine, the path has passed beneath their feet one step at a time. While struggles remain, there have also been marvelous successes, leaving each family member richer and more complete than they otherwise would have been.

One purpose of this book is to help the reader move forward with courage, especially those who find themselves unexpectedly single and raising children. There is reason for hope; you are not broken. There are others out there like you who will understand your complex life and family situation. They will love you and your children for who you are and who you desire to become. Singles without children will also gain insight from these principles should they end up seriously dating a single parent.

A second goal is to help blended families identify and avoid the pitfalls they will face along the way. Simple identification is not enough if the principles are not implemented early in the relationship. If the couple unites their families without employing these or similar principles, their relationship may become impossible to salvage, placing the affected children's difficult lives at even greater risk. Why repeat someone else's mistakes? Learning from the experiences of others is crucial to moving forward. The goal is to allow readers to learn from those shared herein.

The third is to provide hope that every blended family can be successful. The road will be rough but can also be fun and rewarding. Most of all, don't think your situation is the exception and skip ingredients. If the recipe is reasonably followed, the rewards can be incredibly satisfying.

A symphony of beautiful music can emanate from lives that have been filled with pain, uncertainty, and doubt. As parents in a blended family, it is possible for you to create an atmosphere in which each instrument has its own soul-defining solo moments while still contributing to the beauty of the symphonic whole. You may experience differing degrees of success in your family, but the opportunity to apply the principles outlined in this book is a powerful and worthy endeavor. One of the most important voices in our lifetime, Nelson Mandela, spoke of our influence on other people:

> *What counts in life is not the mere fact that*
> *we have lived. It is what difference we have made to*
> *the lives of others that will determine the significance*
> *of the life we lead.*

The truth is every family goes through a blending process that changes them to a greater or lesser degree. In fact, the ability to adjust to new realities is a key to blended family survival. Every reader, regardless of their life situation, should recognize the value of these shared and well-tested ideas.

Your family will one day marvel at the love, peace, and contentment that abides in your home. Sudden change is part of life. It causes disruption. But life can also be full of unconditional love, growth, gratitude, and understanding the ultimate gift of God to mankind.

The Burbidge family is neither unique nor extraordinary. They are regular people, parents with no special training except that which they have learned in the trenches of life. If they can do it, anyone can.

Choose to walk forward together armed with these principles. Your path can lead toward a bright and rewarding future. Your life will be enriched as you come to feel the deeper meaning and greater sense of opportunity and responsibility defined by Mr. Mandela's life and in his words:

> *We can change the world and make it a better place.*
> *It is in your hands…*

The Family Blender

A typical morning in the Burbidge home finds Leah creating her favorite treat, a green smoothie. Spinach, kale, pineapple, a banana, various other frozen or fresh fruits and veggies, and water go into the appliance as separate ingredients. With the flip of a switch and a loud whir, they are transformed into something that none of them could have become alone, a deceptively delicious yet healthy green smoothie.

It is a disruptive process that dramatically changes each unique ingredient. Okay, it never looks as good as it tastes and takes a little getting used to. But the result unites the disparate mix into a delightful and healthy treat that is more than the sum of its individual parts. Amazingly, the unique flavor of each ingredient is identifiably retained. While a gross simplification, this is the perfect mental image of what happens when two families come together. Except the blending takes longer and is infinitely more complex.

Recently, we sat at the kitchen counter sampling Leah's latest smoothie. We pondered our years together and the current status of our blended family of ten children, six grandchildren, two sons-in-law, and five daughters-in-law. It seemed our first meeting occurred only yesterday. In 2004 we had children ranging in age from four to twenty-five, only one of whom was married.

How did we get from there to here? It was probably good that the details of our future path lurked in an impenetrable fog. Knowing now what it has taken to successfully navigate the family blender would have been overwhelming to absorb all at once. Fortunately, life comes in measured portions. This allowed us time to adjust, decreasing the impact of mounting challenges. Blending a family, in our case, turned out to be a massive undertaking. We did not enter our relationship casually, although it was impossible to adequately anticipate the details. After fourteen plus years we recognize our journey is far from complete. We now realize the blending process will continue for generations and into the eternities.

Our path thus far has included bumps and much real-time learning. We have grown to appreciate that a meaningful family experience can be discovered through a disruptive combination of rough patches and smooth glides. Like the ingredients in the blender we all have been changed by the process. Because the changes were experienced together, they resulted in family members becoming something more than we otherwise would have been.

How does a family ensure that the blending process will produce positive results? We believe relating our experience and learnings can provide critical direction on how to wisely proceed. Success is most often found in guidance about how to identify, prepare for, and avoid potential potholes. That is where our book will make a difference. We offer no guarantees or secret formulas. Be assured that a silver bullet solution is the opposite of the process by which blending occurs. Seasoning or aging is necessary to imprint and unify. But there is a positive way forward for each family.

Identifying problems and potential disruptions before the family slams into them is not difficult for aware, engaged, and attentive parents. Once identified, such difficulties can be approached proactively. It is always easier to avoid trouble than to deal with it after it enters your bedroom or calls you on the phone late at night.

Surprisingly, the beauty we celebrate today is more a result of unexpected discoveries intertwined with foundational values than a firm plan or studied parenting. Like a good green smoothie, a careful combination of the ingredients and a high-quality appliance can make all the difference. It takes practice and some experimentation to get the recipe right, but the result is worth it. While it has been demanding and difficult, our life in the family blender has been incredible. We would do it again without condition or change. We are, however, happy to be where we are.

We do not pretend to have written a scholarly journal, nor have we conducted formal academic research beyond that within our own sphere of life. Nevertheless, there is a wealth of supportive data, including the sources cited, that are in tune with the principles discussed. Rather, our effort provides foundational and practical guidance to those who desire to learn from the successful experience of others. We offer these principles based on such experience, for we have learned that hard-won knowledge can be invaluable. It has also become painfully clear over the years that life is too short for each individual to bump around blindly having to learn every lesson for themselves.

How is it possible to condense our experience into a brief list? Is this the right combination for your situation? Family blending is messy. The lines marking the difference between success and struggle often blur in the blended fog of daily life. This is especially true in the moment when trying to keep your head above water. A seemingly endless list of principles danced across our minds as we tried to finalize a few key foundational characteristics upon which any family might build. The ten provided constitute those we believe our readers will find most meaningful and useful.

Each chapter looks at a principle from a variety of angles. These are illustrated using real-life examples. It is our goal to provide a 360-degree view of the power of each principle. They have been forged in the furnace of blended family life. Tailor them to your specific family situation, apply them consistently, and the blended result will appeal to everyone.

We have chosen to set the tone of this book by using consistent terminology to address family circumstances. We generally refer to birth parents or children as *bio*. The terms *step* or *half* are used when necessary, although we personally are uncomfortable with their connotation. The term *first-degree* blended family refers to families where parents bring children to the marriage, producing both bio-, step-, and the potential for half-siblings. When outside authored material is referenced, the original source is included in the listed *Sources* at the end of the book without footnote. We firmly believe the principles presented may be beneficially applied to every kind of family. Therefore, we have not shied away from sharing experiences from our family lives prior to blending when they provide insight into the principles discussed.

If you are contemplating a leap into, or find yourselves already swirling about in, the *family blender,* make sure you have your emotional Dramamine patch behind your ear and enjoy the ride. Please also take time to study the principles we've presented with even greater intensity. They work, they really do.

CHAPTER 1

Everyone Lives in a Blended Family

Historical Blind Spots

It was November 2004. Love was in the air. We were engaged! But something else hovered above us also. Clark was out of work and hustling consulting jobs to pay significant child support and alimony. We had ten children between us, ages four to twenty-five. At least four would be immediately living in our home, while others would come and go. But we had no home and were moving to a new town. This meant changing schools, friends, churches, social, sporting, and other activities.

One son was approaching personal bankruptcy, two others were at risk of failing school, and four of our children were so conflicted that we had no contact. There were three former spouses creating varying degrees of disruption, two sets of in-laws, eight siblings, and a couple of lawyers, all of whom had opinions about what we should or should not do. None of our friends had been through this, and the bookshelves were nearly bare of meaningful blended family literature. What in the world were we thinking?

Does this sound familiar? If it does you have our deepest sympathy, and we are thrilled you found our book. We certainly had some positives going for us that will be discussed later, but that is a fair description of the mountain we faced. Perhaps the biggest problem was that society's recognition of such challenges seemed nearly absent. Acknowledging the existence of a blended family creates numerous questions that few want to hear, and no one wants to answer.

Awareness regarding blended families has dramatically changed within our lifetime. During the 1960s and 1970s, society seemed hesitant to openly discuss the concepts of the untimely death of a spouse, single-parent families, divorce, or step-families. Neither of us could have named a school friend that had a single parent, divorced parents, or was in a stepfamily. Of course, we were not looking for such situations and like most children had limited awareness beyond what kind of cereal was in the pantry or what our friends were doing after school.

When such family circumstances stumbled into the open, they were often treated peripherally or in hushed tones while the subject was awkwardly changed. When Clark was a teen-ager, a close relative divorced. The circumstances were never discussed. It was not until years later when he reached out to his cousins that he gained insight regarding the pain and struggle involved.

Perhaps we were uniquely ignorant youth, but any non-tra-ditional family or the parental situations of our friends simply did not impact us in any way we remember. Sure, we were aware that most of them had two parents in the home. But whether it changed, or some homes had only a single parent simply were not on our radar, let alone the reasons behind such changes or circumstances.

Hollywood provided few resources to help ease the issue into the open. Offerings were limited to superficial comedies like *Cheaper by the Dozen*, *The Parent Trap,* and *Yours, Mine and Ours*. In *The Wizard of Oz,* Dorothy lived with her Auntie Em and Uncle Henry. This was her home according to the ruby slippers. What about her parents? She is referenced as an orphan in literature, but like most pop culture we are steered away from additional insight. We also do not know if she was living with bio-relatives although she calls them Uncle and Aunt. Maybe there is a lot more to the classic theme song *Somewhere Over the Rainbow* than just living in the Kansas dustbowl.

TV was even less enlightening with shows like *My Three Sons*, *The Andy Griffith Show,* and *The Munsters*. The first two were single-parent families with little further information provided. The third was a barely referenced blended family except that the non-monster daughter was the butt of constant jokes because she was different.

As evidence that modern media has not changed much, Hollywood offerings are led by remakes of three movies previously referenced. Additions like *Elf, Blended,* and *Terminator* offer little additional insight.

The TV genre has muddied the concept by making it incidental to extended families, cohabitation, live-in friend relationships, or completely unrelated plot concentrations with *Buffy the Vampire Slayer*, *Full House*, *Two and a Half Men,* and *Modern Family*. Only one of these includes a true first-degree blended family. The primary reason for singleness is usually the more sympathetic death of a spouse. To be fair, there is a somewhat more open treatment of issues. But, like the older offerings, they tend to be generic family issues or skewed toward modern pop culture social interests. The blended family seems to have been leap-frogged by more politically attractive focuses.

If you would have asked a teenage Clark what he thought about the subject of blended families, his first response would likely have been to reference a weekly sitcom, *The Brady Bunch*. We apologize if the theme song gets stuck in your head the rest of the day.

Think about *The Brady Bunch*. A couple gets married and each brings three children to the new family. It remains one of the few shows about a true first-degree blended family. The dynamics of the situation could have provided years of interesting and dramatic viewing. It could have been the first reality television program. But this was a situation comedy. Serious, in-depth portrayal of social issues was ground waiting to be broken by others such as the writers of *MASH* and *All in the Family*.

Each week there were superficial issues that promoted stereotypes. Characters primarily dealt with legitimate problem-solving typical of all families with children. Furthermore, it usually got neatly tied up in less than thirty minutes including commercials. The fact that they were a blended family rarely, if ever, made it past the opening credits.

The genre is further diluted by the countless movies and fairy tales emphasizing wicked stepmother or evil stepfather characters. Included are some of the most endearing children's animated feature films of all time. This misdirection creates false perceptions about behaviors that complicate application of the ten principles.

Why has society been hesitant to enter into serious public dialogue? Could it be that speaking about blended families leads one down the path to dealing with the uncomfortable causes of single parenthood? Death, unwed or absentee parents, abandonment, abuse, serial cohabitation, and divorce involve stories generally disturbing to most people.

Relating the story behind the circumstance is often painful and awkward to those involved. Families do not generally talk about this over dinner. Friends avoid such conversations and shrink from hearing the gory details.

The trend among news outlets has more recently been to glorify the single-parent or alternative lifestyle as a courageous new choice, treating the circumstance as if it might be preferable. We certainly are not suggesting that single parents or alternative unions cannot be heroic or worthy of our love and support. However, asserting they are a wise or preferable choice to be sought when statistically more healthy and secure options are available is either naïve or influenced by an agenda

It is gratifying that literature on blended families is becoming more available. There certainly should be more. Each family situation is different. Its unique aspects vary based on individual backgrounds and how the blended family was established. It is often the case that careless initial steps can stack the deck against success before the family gets started. We are enthusiastic about sharing the perspective we have gained from navigating the rocks and shoals inside the blender itself.

Elusive Awareness

What is a blended family anyway? Certainly *The Brady Bunch* qualifies. Leah grew up in a blended family, but she never viewed it as such. Her biological father and mother divorced when she was an infant. Her mother remarried, and Leah was adopted by a man whom she always considered her biological father. She has a bio-sister and five half-siblings, yet she never considered herself part of a blended family. The environment of love and devotion created by her parents was successful in Leah's case. She remembers her youth on the Pacific coast of Oregon being as normal as any of her peers.

Modern social media has produced an important change in our children's awareness versus our own at the same age. Our teenage daughter knows the family situations of her friends. She plays an informal role with several helping them deal with difficult situations. This includes friends visiting our home for meals, family activities, lessons, study or prayer times, comfort, and counsel. Young people benefit greatly from a safe harbor. It should be in their own home. But when that isn't possible, they naturally seek a place where they can feel safe, valued, and cared about.

If a positive alternative is unavailable, a counterfeit may be found. Without a healthy safe harbor and engaged parental guidance, youth are at risk of sliding onto dark paths involving drugs, alcohol, trouble in school or with the law, and rebellious or immoral behavior. Such involvement may offer temporary escape in exchange for a downward spiral in self-image, confidence, and esteem. They may turn to destructive behaviors for short-term escape that ultimately produce additional burdens, pain, and remorse. Self-discipline and freedom often become the ultimate casualties. Providing safe spaces can allow young people to get their bearings.

It is not uncommon for our daughter to come home with questions or requests for help from friends. Our desire to reach out to such youth and their families is an example of a principle that will be discussed later.

Becoming a parent and taking on the responsibility is a biological process with legal ramifications. However, becoming a mother or father to that child is something much more. The title of mother or father is earned through years of compassion, commitment, and unconditional love. These are titles given by those you parent, not forcefully assumed. They entail much more than a legal or biological act.

Clark grew up in a traditional home with two parents. Alcoholism and possible PTSD tore at the fabric of their family life for his first twenty years. His parents struggled to overcome the demons at the gate. Despite a few critical periods, they remained devoted to each other until they succeeded. It made the remaining years of their family experience all the more sacred. His father died in 1998, and his mother remarried a few years later. His stepfather's wife had also passed away. Both had extended families of married children and numerous grandchildren.

This counts as a blended family, yet Clark never considered this beyond his mother being remarried. Even though he and his bio-siblings were in their forties with families, he remembers siblings on both sides having difficulty adjusting. But there was no conscious realization he had become part of a blended family.

We had both experienced divorce before meeting. Leah had been single longer at the time we met. She was already aware of the associated challenges. She had four boys from her first marriage and a four-year-old daughter from her second marriage. Clark had three girls and two boys from his marriage. It was not until we found ourselves seriously dating each other that we began to acknowledge the demands of our prospective blended family.

Why do situations like this seem to sneak up on a couple? The elephant in the living room is impossible to ignore. Yet it caught us by surprise as our relationship became serious. Herein lies the blind spot with individuals and society. Too often, people whose lives are touched by family blending do not consciously acknowledge its implications. It is also easy to underestimate the demands that will result from a blending decision. Certainly, there must be important learning from such experiences. But the principles seem to be compartmentalized and difficult to access.

The Data Speaks

Before bringing the foundational principles to light, let us take a moment to set the stage regarding the realities we deal with in today's society. Certainly, we should all be better prepared to enter the family blender. But why be concerned? Aren't the chances we will end up in the blender unlikely? There is in fact a high likelihood that every reader will have a brush with the blender during their lives. Let us then address the most basic question. How pervasive are blended families?

Provided below is a brief overview of the current state of families, marriage, and children based on numerous studies and census information. The facts are difficult to ignore. Data presented below rely heavily on compilations provided by the National Stepfamily Resource Center (NSRC). We are grateful to the NSRC for organizing critical information in an easily understandable and accessible format.

Provided below is a brief overview of the current state of families, marriage, and children based on numerous studies and census information. The facts are difficult to ignore. Data presented below rely heavily on compilations provided by The Step Family Foundation, and the National Stepfamily Resource Center (NSRC). We are grateful to these organizations providing critical information in an easily understandable and accessible format.

The fact is that even our government has shied away from details in these areas. Perhaps they remain uncomfortable with the stigma associated with acknowledging such challenges in society. The NSRC in their November *2015 Stepfamily Fact Sheet* and Stepfamily Foundation updates through 2021 assert that they have used many of their own studies because of deficiencies in those provided by the government. Although, it is important to note that some of the data below does appear on the US Census Bureau reports. The NSRC caveats the US government information by pointing out:

"The U.S. Census Bureau recently decided to discontinue providing estimates of marriage, divorce, and remarriage except for those that are available from our current census. Thus, many of our current estimates were derived from ... earlier data sources."

Current marriage demographic estimates:

- 43% - 50% of all first marriages end in divorce within the first 15 years.

- 1,300 new stepfamilies are forming every day.

- Over 50% of all US families are remarried or re-coupled.

- 60% of those remarried or re-coupled break up when children are involved.

- 25% of all men and women report being married two or more times by age 50.

- Of those divorced, 75% remarry and 65% bring children from a previous union.

- 60% of those who get remarried or re-coupled, break up whether or not children are involved.

- The average length of first time and remarriages is about the same at 8 years.

- The probability of remarriage has been trending downward since the 1970s.

- NSRC suggests that given current trends, 33-50% of youth will have been part of a stepfamily by 18 years of age.

- According to The Stepfamily Foundation's research, more than 60% of divorced fathers visit their children. These children do not legally "reside" with their fathers. So, neither government, nor academic research includes these fathers and their children as stepfamilies! The father may be a single dad, but most likely he is re-coupled or remarried, thus creating a stepfamily. These children shuttle between their parent's homes, radically increasing the numbers of stepfamilies. These fathers are ignored and uncounted.

- 75% of stepfamilies complain of "not having access to resources as a stepfamily.

- 50% of the women and 30% of the men were still intensely angry with their former spouses.

Information on American children under 18 years of age from the 2009 and 2022 *Current Population Study (CPS)*:

- 30.2% and 29.8% of children live with one parent or other relatives. Trend slightly down.

- 2.8% and 6.8% of children living with two parents live with two cohabitating, not married parents. Trend up 242%.

- 12.3% of children living with two parents are part of a stepfamily. The 2022 Census does not have information identifying status as a Stepfamily.

To be clear, this means that approximately 48.9% (up from 45.3% ten years ago) of children in the US live with a single parent, relatives, or in a two-parent blended family. That is nearly half, and it doesn't count children of blended or single-parent families that are clearly affected but are not living in the home nor does it currently include stepfamilies as an easily identifiable category. For example, when we married, seven of our ten children would not have been considered to have been part of a blended family because they were over eighteen and/or not living at the blended family home location. Therefore, they would have been excluded from the statistics.

This fact alone begs to be printed in bold front-page headlines. The superficial blended family treatment in media, movies, and TV programs pales in comparison to our government's own apparent disinterest and negligent accounting. It is beyond belief that our own census statistics would not recognize as part of blended families those children who are not physically living in the blended home. In addition, it breaks our hearts to think that children eighteen and older are also ignored as if they were nonexistent. These children will certainly have interaction and feel the effects. They generally have visitation, vacations, and holidays that bring them into close association with their stepsiblings and family. The challenges and adjustments are just as real regardless of their age or custodial circumstances, sometimes even greater.

Pew Research Center 2010 and 2015 Estimates:

- 42% of adults have at least one step relative.

- 54% of children do not live in a two parent first marriage.

- 30% of adults have a stepsibling or half-sibling.

- 52% of people under the age of 30 have a step relative and 44% of those have a stepsibling or half-sibling.

- 60% of African Americans have a step relative and 45% report having a stepsibling or half-sibling.

- 39% of Caucasians have a step relative and 26% report having a stepsibling or half-sibling.

- 70% of African American children live in a remarriage, cohabitating, or single parent family. This is compared to 52% of Hispanic, 44% of Caucasian, and 27% of Asian children.

- 71% of African American births are to unmarried women. This is compared to 53% of Hispanic, and 29% Caucasian births. Overall, 40% of all births in the US are to unmarried women. This is up 17.5% since 2000.

In other words, the situation is pervasive and becoming more common.

The NSRC includes two interesting footnotes to clarify the inherent understatement in available blended family statistics:

- "To date, government reporting of population figures indicates families in which the child resides. So, if the child lives with a divorced, single parent and the other nonresident parent has remarried, the child is not included in the calculations as being a member of a stepfamily."

- "Children who are 18 and older or no longer living at home are not included in estimations."

This means that the number of children in blended families easily exceeds the 52% level reported by the Pew Research Center. Given the above statistic that 75% of divorced parents remarry and the non-counting of children over the age of 18, the true percentage of those with step or half-relatives could be much higher. In our case, they missed 70% of our children.

Other credible and well-researched sources provide the following perspective:

- 37% of all families are single parent.

- 40% of all children are born outside of wedlock.

- Divorce and out-of-wedlock births cost state and local government $112 billion per year.

- 40% of all children will live in a cohabitating home at some point in their life.

- Serial transitions in to and out of relationships are now typical in the USA and have serious consequences for children.

One can conclude from the data available that blended families are common and increasing as a percent of society. Further research into the source material reveals a critical need for providing a positive environment for children affected by the root issues that bring about single parenting and potential blended families. Some of the highest risk factors for children occur as a direct result of the root causes.

Children of divorced parents are at significantly higher risk to become involved with drugs, have difficulty in school, and run-ins with law enforcement than children in a traditional two- parent family with a father and a mother. These risk rates are also higher than in children of widowed parents. Such factors produce a wide range of behavioral problems, poverty, and disconnection from the non-present parent (typically the father), insecurity, and life disruptions.

There is also a growing epidemic of fathers absent from the home. Single-parent families are five times more likely to be headed by a mother than a father and the Pew Research and other studies have concluded that two parent families where both parents are of the same gender have essentially the same risk rates as single parent families. The National Fatherhood Initiative provides the following sobering statistics in their current updates:

- 25% of children in America live in a home without a father (The highest among the 27 industrialized countries surveyed.) and 72% of black children in America live in a home without a father. This has risen steadily since the mid-1960s.

- Children who grow up without a father are:

400% as likely to live in poverty

700% as likely to experience teen pregnancy

More likely to have behavioral problems

More likely to face abuse and neglect

200% as likely to die as an infant

More likely to abuse drugs and alcohol

More likely to serve time in prison

200% as likely to suffer obesity

More likely to become involved in committing crimes

200% as likely to drop out of high school

Family blending, if done well and developed wisely, can help reverse this trend. It brings the critical influence of a father and mother working together back into children's lives. To begin addressing this profound need, we must first recognize that blended families are more common than most realize.

Imagine an auditorium with one thousand randomly chosen people from a broad strip of society. The speaker asks everyone to stand, then invites all those who have a stepparent or stepsiblings or half-siblings to sit down. Between three and four hundred of those present would sit. Another one hundred and twenty would be asked to sit because they have a close step relative. This is evidence enough of the pervasiveness of blended families in our culture. However, our imaginary speaker throws a curveball to all those who remain standing, causing them to sit, thus proving that none are untouched by blended family circumstances. What would that unhittable curveball be?

The speaker looks over those who remain standing and invites everyone who has in-laws or whose parents have in-laws to sit. Why ask that question? It is relevant because anytime a couple gets married, it involves two families blending through in-laws and their extended families. This means the need to blend different upbringings, traditions, expectations, socio-economic backgrounds, personalities, demands, and cultures. In addition, differing religions, languages, and races are also more commonly in play than in the past. These factors also meet the definition of blending even though the daily dynamics may be reduced versus that of a first-degree blended family with children. The bottom line is that no one is left standing.

You Can Do It!

The following chapters contain principles that apply to and can be used successfully by all families. We are confident that every reader will find these principles difference-makers in their family situation. However, our primary focus is on the *first-degree* blended family.

Successful family blending is tough. The needs and vigilance of a regular family are infinitely magnified for those engaged in *first-degree* blending. Establishing any family and developing relationships with the extended family is going to have its good and bad days. There may be noise or interference from former spouses or extended families. These principles will help your family fight through the noise and build healthy, collective, and individual behaviors.

Your family can do much more than survive. Work to achieve a joyous, thriving, uplifting atmosphere where every family member has an opportunity to reach his or her greatest potential. Create a strong, happy, wise, and emotionally healthy foundation that will bless your children. Such a goal is within every family's reach. It is worth every tear, every prayer, every effort, every late night, and every sacrifice. It will make demands on you that will change the way you live. You can do it. The following chapters provide a framework that will get you there together.

CHAPTER II

Principle #1: No Surprises

Volcanos and Earthquakes

Leah grew up in Astoria, Oregon. It is a moderate-sized fishing town and art colony on the west coast of Oregon where the Columbia River meets the Pacific Ocean. The Lewis & Clark Expedition arrived at the West Coast nearby. There is a large obelisk called the Column that rises 125 feet above the ridge in the center of the old town. A spiraling staircase of 164 steps takes one to the small observation deck, which offers a breathtaking 360-degree panorama of the surrounding countryside for more than one hundred miles. Standing at the top looking northeast is sobering. A single prominent feature dominates that quarter of the view—the fractured remains of the Mt. Saint Helens volcano. The explosion of Mt. Saint Helens was a worldwide event in May 1980 when Leah was attending Astoria High.

It was foreshadowed by nearly two months of earthquakes and other geological changes. These included a rising magma dome that scientists warned would produce an eruption. The area surrounding the volcano was evacuated. Still, fifty-seven people perished when the massive explosion blew out the northeastern side of the mountain. Among the victims were several individuals who refused to heed the mounting signs. The fact that it exploded was not a surprise, but its magnitude, destruction, and global effects were.

Fortunately for Leah and the town of Astoria, the volcano blew out in the other direction. However, she recalls everything being covered by a layer of ash. Her father worked for the US Forest Service and remembers how the extremely fine ash powder worked its way into everything. "It was in the drinking water, homes, hair, skin, and food. Its microscopic particles caused problems with vehicles, hand tools, and every kind of machinery." This made cleanup more difficult, hampering regular operations for weeks. Her mother related that it changed how she lived. Life's regular concerns faded into the background as she lived each day with a surrealistic edge of "… increased awareness and heightened senses waiting for something else to happen."

Clark lived through a number of large earthquakes in Los Angeles, California. He noticed in others a curious reaction. Such sudden changes disrupt us from our daily routine of relative sameness leaving some jumpy or anxious for weeks. Something as simple as a truck driving down the street can set off the adrenal glands. Most people recovered over the ensuing days or weeks, but some were changed for long periods.

One young mother in his neighborhood required her children to sleep with her under the dining room table for months following a particularly strong quake. She was so traumatized by the increased intensity of the shaking experienced on the second level of their two-story home that they sold it and moved to a single-level, ranch-style home. Natural events like these are instructive in understanding similar reactions found in family crises.

Life-Changing Events

Nobody likes surprises. This is especially true when a life-changing event occurs. A marriage that blends two families together changes every involved person's life. Imagine the children trying to become comfortable with a stranger hanging out with their mom or dad. That is tough enough by itself. Then comes the shocker; that person is going to be married to your bioparent and living in your house! Add the emotions that go with split loyalties and occasional manipulation by former spouses. Consider changes in schedules and meeting the new person's children, who also may suddenly be moving in. What about differences in discipline or interaction?

If that is not sufficient disruption in a child's life, pile on a move to a new house, new neighborhood, different school or church, and having to make new friends. Occasionally, this may mean relocating to a different city or state. Visitation may be disrupted, producing court proceedings. Then imagine the blended parents having a baby, creating potential for further self-doubt, envy, or insecurity. Picture all this happening in addition to the parents appearing to not be making any material commitment except to move in together. Children are perceptive. Why should they be expected to make a commitment to this seemingly careless new arrangement when their parents are not? A dating couple with children can never approach their relationship in a vacuum. That is a recipe for another separation or divorce.

Contemplating the list of real and potential disruptions makes us shudder. How do children deal with all that at the same time? Almost every element of the support structure they have ever known is suddenly swept away in a near perfect storm.

The landscape with which they were familiar is forever changed. The fine powder of events seeps into every aspect of their thinking, causing difficulty with recovering the machinery of life for months, years, and sometimes forever.

One of our sons who is now married and in his mid-twenties shared this perspective. He related that he had moved so many times and attended so many schools that he never felt like he was able to develop lasting friendships. "It created a hole in my life," he concluded. It doesn't matter whether or not this was a completely accurate statement of what he went through. Perception can often rule over reality and needs to be treated seriously even if the parent's observation differs. He stated that it was not until we married that he found stability, friends, and began to blossom. His unspoken *thank you* became a tender moment for both of us.

Can you imagine what this change does to young people? Everything they knew is gone, and in its place, nothing. By nothing we mean a completely empty slate waiting for new stories to be written about new places, friends, and experiences. This can become a wonderful fresh start providing an uplifting adventure for the children in the long run. Nevertheless, it presents a difficult challenge getting them to a place where they can view it rationally. Children are resilient, but they are not superhuman. Changing everything in their lives at the same time creates potential for desperation that can produce significant behavioral changes.

Empowerment Through Communication

An initial negative reaction is understandable. But there is much that parents can do to avoid making it harder. Parents need to start early in preparing the family for such an advent. There must be patience in dealing with the rough patches that result. Knowing that you are in it together helps. Having a common belief system, as discussed in chapter nine, is fundamental. Taking the time to work with each of your children will smooth the adjustment.

However, surprising children by courting or making these premarital and post-marital decisions off their radar can seriously damage relationship trust. Failure to properly approach such remarriage disruptions can become a major obstacle to the blended family's ultimate success. A couple must resist the temptation to downplay developing relationship plans or dive headlong into sudden and careless physical involvement, loose commitment, or cohabitation. Of course, it makes the courting process more complex by involving the children. But open communication also avoids long-term adjustment and behavioral problems. Real life is messy and takes a lot of effort. Family blending is definitely not for those who are unwilling to communicate with all their heart, might, mind, and strength and put in the extra work that is absolutely required.

Be completely open. Involve the children in searching for a new home. If you are moving to a home already occupied by your spouse-to-be, involve your children in the due diligence on schools, churches, and the community. If your children have specific activities in which they are involved such as sports teams, music, dance, scouting, etc., then include them in checking out available options in the new location. Perhaps their future stepsiblings can assist in the transition by providing introductions or showing them around.

Even if your new spouse and their children move into your home, you can expect difficulties with your own transition. Of course, you may expect transitional growing pains with your spouse's children as they adjust to the new location as mentioned above. You may even experience territorial and turf battles within the walls of your own home. Who sleeps where? Whose room is this now? Where do my things go? Sharing space, toys, and parents is the fine powder of change in everything.

If handled together and in a healthy way, there will be opportunities for your children to draw hopeful conclusions for themselves. The process will also promote conversations between parents and children about what is going on. They will gain a sense of respect that their voices are being heard.

You should expect emotions during the process. However, if you respect the children, your example will rub off. Respect is most visible to children in the way a parent listens and communicates. To do it well requires time. It cannot be rushed.

By showing respect and encouraging input, you naturally help them feel more confident. They will begin to sense that there is a place for them in the new situation. Your children need to know that they are an important part of your plans rather than mere baggage or an afterthought. No parent tries to make their children feel that way, but kids are perceptive and quickly draw their own conclusions. Before you are aware, your own behavior may result in a child beginning their own process of self-labeling as invisible or unwanted.

Quality interaction and respect, on the other hand, help children learn that you share many of their concerns. The *ah-ha* moment comes when they recognize everyone is in this together and progress can only be made as a team. This is a precedent that will pay big dividends later on when the dust clears. Building this trust becomes even more critical when parents begin dealing with family rules, behavior expectations, and consequences.

Sometimes, in spite of all you do, a child will continue to believe you don't care or didn't listen. At these times, personal, patient interaction focused on love and support will help rebuild critical structure in their lives. On a couple of occasions, we have reminded a child that even though the results were not precisely what they had in mind, it didn't mean that we failed to understand their point of view. Disagreements happen. Parents contribute to this positively when they refrain from dictating and remain open to ideas. Helping children recognize they also have an important role allows them to feel like they are part of the solution. This kind of family dynamic allows virtually every issue to be worked through. Parents must be committed to invest significant time and attention in this effort.

Another common challenge comes when children are out of the house. They are less affected by some of the changes previously discussed. However, they remain sensitive to time and attention from their bio-parent. This may change, making them wary of the new spouse. Take time to meet with them where possible. Ongoing communication will be helpful in smoothing over their concerns. Help them feel like they are also a respected part of the process. As adults they may have suggestions or advice that will help parents in their blended family efforts.

However, at the end of the day, the soon-to-be-married couple cannot and should not attempt to please everybody. You do the best you can. Recognize that some relationships may take longer than others. Based on an atmosphere of respect, communication, and engagement, you proceed, knowing you have done all you can and that you will never give up. Family blending takes effort. If a couple is unwilling to put in the effort, do not jump into the blender.

A New Normal?

When we were dating, it became clear that our marriage would produce sweeping changes in the lives of our children. We agreed that we would look for a new home and that Clark would sell his existing home. We found a home near Clark's new job, and Leah and her children moved in a month before the marriage. Clark continued in his previous location until after the marriage. The new home was a thirty-minute drive from where Leah had previously rented. That meant a new neighborhood, school, church, friends, scout troop, sports teams, and seemingly countless other variables. Further, this all happened right after the Christmas holiday, midway through the school year. In retrospect, we probably couldn't have picked a more difficult time to change everything that mattered in our lives.

How would it impact our children and family dynamics? How would it affect self-esteem, school performance, behavior, and long-term quality of life? We might have made the perfect case study for placing children in an at-risk environment. Yet, all five of Leah's disrupted children remain within the family circle. We have also maintained warm relationships and regular communication with those who are now older and on their own.

Clark's children were married, in college, or living with their bio-mother. They faced an entirely different set of circumstances that put them at risk in no-less-real ways, such as having placed upon them severe loyalty pressure to avoid associating with the new blended family. The result was a double task of trying to help five of our children adjust to their dad's new living circumstances while at the same time patiently dealing with the obstacles thrown in their path. All of this was necessary while working toward a normal, healthy level of communication with all our children. This severely tested dynamics within our new family. One could have reasonably asked, "Why would we put them through it?" or "Why didn't we lose them all?"

There are numerous answers, but one stands above the rest. We recognized the truth. We were building from scratch and could not assume anything would be predictable based on the past. The cornerstones of our approach became respect, clear communication, patience, unconditional love, strong acts of commitment and a clear and consistent set of spiritual values. This allowed us to exercise faith in the ultimate outcome, knowing that we were never alone. Each of the children living with us were included in the decision-making process.

Schools and neighborhoods were discussed, feedback encouraged, and we listened. There were still surprises; there always are in life. But we worked to minimize the frequency and degree of those that occurred. The children not in the home were reached out to and drawn into the family, to the extent possible, with the same warm welcome, respect, patience, and communication.

Our children also knew their parents were on the same page with the same ultimate goals. It allowed our children to more easily trust and ultimately buy into the new situation. Can you imagine the instability that would have been injected into this already fragile situation had we chosen to casually begin cohabitating without any defining commitment? We understand it can be difficult to trust in a long-term commitment for a couple who have experienced previous emotional trauma. One or both may be hesitant based on previous bad experiences including divorce or death. Nevertheless, test driving each other and the relationship through a casual cohabitation style commitment often leads to children looking for stability outside the home or acting out. It is a common reason for strife and a risk for ultimate blended family failure.

It is amazing how difficult challenges become simpler and obstacles more easily overcome when a couple stands together. It is also striking to note how even the smallest decisions become impossibly difficult when a couple is not on the same page. There will be more discussion of what it means to be on the same page in a later chapter.

Compromise and Discovery

Our children felt this unity of purpose and bought in. We compromised on some things like bringing the trampoline with us and getting a small house dog. It would have been easy to say no to some of these changes. In fact, we harbored some serious reservations, particularly about the dog. There were family discussions about looking for dogs that had minimal shedding and a non-barky temperament.

The dog decision involved some incredibly professional lobbying by our children led by one of our sons. This was a moment of truth for us since we had previously agreed that we would not have pets in the home given all the other variables with which we were dealing. Clark would have preferred fish and Leah a parakeet. A dog was something else altogether in our minds. Life was busy enough. Leah was the first to cave and was able to convince Clark that under specific conditions things could be manageable. There were pie-crust promises made by the children that they would take care of the dog. Famous last words like, "You won't even know it's here!" were uttered. Some of them were honored, but Leah was primarily saddled with much of the additional care.

We reviewed various studies indicating pets help children and adults manage the stress of difficult transitions. For example, simply petting a dog releases feel-good endorphins. We settled on a mini-pincher we named Shadow. He became a perfect addition to our family and helped each of us deal with our own individual healing processes in ways we had not anticipated.

Life decisions tend to produce results that fall somewhere between one's hopes and fears. We had both in this case, but in the end our family has been blessed, and all the changes, even the small ones, impacted the outcome for good.

Parenting older children presented a different challenge. Clark has often stated, only partly tongue-in-cheek, that "parents don't really begin parenting until their children turn eighteen." Of course, this is not when parenting starts. But it definitely creates additional requirements. Once your children become adults you must learn to parent by consent. This means your influence becomes more permission and respect based, often limited to example and advice. Such advice provided is more effective when it is consented to or asked for.

When we were married, we had the support of Clark's oldest son and his wife. However, his other four children were not in a position to have an open relationship without risking a severely negative reaction from their bio-mother. This took time and patience. Two of the four have chosen to reopen their relationships with us. A third has made great strides evidenced by increased confidence in communication and interaction. They have enriched their own lives and all of ours by doing so. It is an ongoing process where each one must move at their own individual pace.

The Tipping Point

There comes a tipping point in any newly developing relationship. It is a critical moment when you must decide if you are all-in or not. For us it came as the 2004 Thanksgiving weekend approached, four and a half months after our first meeting. We felt committed to the concept of marriage and a blended family, but we had not announced anything. Four of Clark's children, as previously discussed, remained heavily conflicted. Clark's attorney counseled that we should wait to make an announcement until after the situation had settled down. It was a difficult moment, and the attorney's advice needed to be weighed carefully.

We discussed the situation. Leah's children were completely on board as was Clark's oldest son. But there was a risk that getting engaged would potentially create an even greater rift or provide additional opportunities for any who wished to drive a wedge between Clark and his other children.

Leah was supportive but allowed Clark to work through the decision since its potential effects would play out regarding his bio-children. She knew he had to arrive at his own commitment on the subject. We prayed, considered alternative paths, and decided to go ahead. There remained much pressure to wait, but finally we came to an important realization. The attorney's counsel was not about delaying an engagement announcement a couple of weeks. It was about not getting married for months, years, or at all. We decided that we could see no clear path that the situation with Clark's children would change.

We concluded that the stability and happiness our marriage would create was more likely to increase a healthy atmosphere and promote healing going forward. In addition, it seemed clear that we had done all we could.

Perhaps it was rationalization, but we decided to follow the spiritual impressions in our hearts. It was the supreme test of our commitment. Once we announced our engagement, we were all-in. We also discovered a groundswell of support and well-wishers confirming our decision. We may never know to what extent it affected Clark's children, but those who have re-opened their relationship with us have never mentioned it as an obstacle. Reason and logic can only take a couple so far in making decisions. There comes a point where it fails, leaving a commitment-laced leap of faith. We took that leap together with our heavenly Father and it has made all the difference.

Family life cannot be wrapped up, explained, or under-stood in neat packaging. If there were a manual, it would have to be dynamic with constantly adjusting pages, diagrams, and descriptions. The process of creating a blended family is full of sudden change, unexpected adventure, and unforeseen twists. Avoiding unnecessary surprises that disrupt lives will always smooth the way. Your blended family adventure will include an ample supply of joy, sorrow, satisfaction, and frustration. And, in spite of your best efforts, there will still be surprises. But every bump and dip will be more easily absorbed by creating an environment where respect, communication, engagement, love, patience, and especially faith reign. You can demonstrate to your children every day that their home is a safe harbor with committed parents who are on the same page.

CHAPTER III

Principle #2: It Starts Now

How it Started

We met through an online dating website that reflected our values, interests, and beliefs in early July 2004. It was a strange new experience for Clark who had no previous exposure to online dating. At the time Leah had been online for a couple of years and was familiar with how the sites worked. We both learned that being suddenly single made us pet projects for several friends and family members. It seems that everyone knows someone who sells insurance, and everyone also knows someone who is single and looking for a relationship. It can be a tremendous distraction.

Nowadays it is difficult for a single parent to effectively date without some online component. Both of us decided to do our own online searches to help protect our sanity and independence. We also discovered very quickly that online dating provided access to people we would not otherwise have met.

We came across each other in a nearly simultaneous manner. Clark was advised by well-meaning friends to check out an online dating site. He didn't anticipate becoming part of the site. However, he discovered that a prerequisite to doing a free search was completing a profile and uploading a picture. He did so and began the search. The selected parameters produced three-hundred profiles. He reviewed them on a holiday and bookmarked only six, one of which was Leah. What he didn't realize was that the owner of every profile on which he clicked received an email informing them that he had done so.

In addition, any person bookmarked got an email stating that he had identified her as a *favorite*. Clark unknowingly sent out over three-hundred introductory or favorite emails. He didn't think to check his email again until the end of the long weekend. He was inundated with responses and tried to politely answer each one, which was like pouring gasoline on a fire.

Leah identified him on the new members list and flagged his profile. She almost immediately received an email that Clark had marked her as a favorite. A few introductory emails were exchanged, which led to phone conversations. One of our favorite early phone calls occurred when Leah gave Clark a color test. This is a series of questions that, based on answers, classify a person as one of four colors—red, blue, white, or yellow— some more compatible than others and all having a list of personality traits. She discovered he was a compatible color. More importantly, we learned a lot about each other answering the questions and laughing until our sides hurt. After several more emails and phone conversations, we arranged to meet at a local dance for single adults.

Our first in-person interaction set the stage for our courtship. Leah already had a date for the dance, and her date had rules. They could each dance with others, but they had agreed to dance all slow dances together. Clark thought it would be fun to send her a tongue-in-cheek legal contract promising to respect her date's rules. Leah responded with an equally tongue-in-cheek agreement consenting to his proposal. The night of the dance arrived, and Clark realized he only knew her first name and online handle, which was *Highspirited*. By the time he arrived, the crowd was too large and music too loud to find her.

Clark approached the DJ requesting that he make an announcement: "Will Leah Highspirited please come to the DJ's desk. Your party is here to meet you." Surprisingly, it worked. Leah came forward and the dancing began. We enjoyed four dances. Then came the slow dance, and she reluctantly honored the promise made to her date. That was it. Clark stood watching her disappear into the crowd feeling like Prince Charming having lost his Cinderella without even a glass slipper to show for it. Leah also remembers feeling sad about having to go back to her date.

During the next few weeks, there were longer conversations, a lunch date, emails, and another singles dance interaction with no competing date rules. Within a month we had transitioned into our first real date. We soon began to realize something special was developing. By the end of September, we both felt marriage was in our future. Our engagement was announced just before Thanksgiving, and we were married in mid-February 2005, just over seven months after our first online interaction.

The brief calendaring provided above does not begin to describe the process through which we passed. There is an emotional roller coaster involved in developing strong mutual feelings. But this process also included tough questions we had to ask each other and equally challenging ones raised by others. The risks were made all too obvious by the dynamics of our complex family situations mixed with the emotions of falling in love. It was a wild ride that only Mr. Toad could truly have appreciated.

Yet, through it all, we felt guided by the spirit of a loving God. There was a feeling of rightness in our developing relationship. We look back on it now and wonder why we decided to take it on and how we successfully navigated through. The answer we always get is that it happened one step at a time, together with the Holy Spirit as our guide. We are still taking it step-by-step, hand-in-hand.

Early Decisions Matter

There were a few decisions we made early in our courtship that had a huge impact. You know, the kind of decisions that seem inconsequential at the time, but in retrospect were foundational. Such decisions made together sometimes stare you in the face as a natural part of moving forward. Others are what we call *almost didn'ts*. These were decisions that we almost didn't make because neither of us appreciated their significance.

Yet with years of perspective, the impact is clear and overwhelming. Perhaps it's best that we do not usually see the most important decisions as being as significant as they are. Had we known then what we see clearly now, the stress could have easily deterred us from the path. The happiness we have found not just today, but along the way from there to here, might never have happened.

There were formidable circumstances that attended our blossoming relationship. Each of us had complex dynamics with former spouses. Our children were dealing with mixed loyalties, which included varying degrees of emotional and behavioral stress. Some were acting out, creating additional burdens for themselves and those around them. Our social, financial, and work situations had been badly disrupted. The environment in which we began the foundation of our family relationship was not remotely conducive to successful growth.

However, against the odds and in spite of numerous obstacles, strong feelings developed. How could our relationship survive the trials that lay ahead? We were focused on the depth and strength of our relationship. Like so many in love, we believed that such feelings combined with faith could overcome anything. As we discussed the principles to include in this book, this one was immediately obvious. In practice it seemed to have naturally fallen into place through collective instinct.

We marvel at our divinely nudged process combined with some critical guiding principles. How did we make it this far when so many flounder? Social media is full of desperate posts and instant-everything crying out for help. The common complaint repeats endlessly as couples drift into live-in blended relationships haphazardly with differing or minimal levels of commitment, expectations, effort, interest, or standards. Wedges can develop quickly, becoming insurmountable problems. A weak foundation and careless beginning can sometimes be corrected, but more often they lead to frustration, disillusionment, and separation. There are simple answers, but they quickly become complex. When we hear these sad stories, we ask ourselves how and where they could have begun differently. Once the downward spiral is in process, momentum tends to take on a life of its own. But there is a way. That is why these principles lived from the start are irreplaceable.

Starting Now

We didn't just date each other, rather we made efforts to develop relationships with the children. You could say that we dated each other's entire family to the extent we could. This became a delicately balanced symphony where each instrument needed its solo moment but was also equally respected for its contribution to the whole.

We call this *starting now* during the dating process. It is not dissimilar in spirit to the process a young couple goes through. Early in their relationship they meet each other's parents and begin to develop healthy extended family relationships in parallel with their own. It is common for parents in such circumstances to provide feedback. In our situation we also received feedback from our children, friends, and extended family members—many of whom acted as self-appointed gatekeepers. We learned to listen but not be overwhelmed by the many voices and often strong opinions.

When two individuals with children begin dating, it usually involves complex dynamics. We discovered two keys: first, take into account where each child stands regarding parental dating. Where are they prepared to begin? It is critical to start from where they are rather than where the couple's relationship expectations are. Second, allow each child to grow with the relationship to the extent they are able or willing. Patience is critical; it cannot be forced.

Everything within reason should be done to allow the child to join the party. Still, one or more children may choose not to participate. The couple may decide to move ahead anyway. In doing so they must continue to work with the non-engaged child. Be realistic and recognize that without a change, it could present a major obstacle to family unity and marital happiness. On the other hand, moving forward to create something stable may be what draws the child in.

For example, Leah had four children in the home. She chose not to have in-depth discussions with them about her dating activities. However, she allowed it to be in the open and answered questions as they arose. There is a delicate balance of inclusion without the burden of stress that often accompanies early dates. She carefully nourished their involvement. We spent a lot of family time together. When the time came, they were happy to welcome Clark into the family. How does a couple make this a smooth and natural process?

There may be obstacles thrown up by one or more of the children. These are understandable and will likely take differing periods of time to overcome. Some may be successfully dealt with in a conversation. Some require days or months of nourishment and confidence building. Still others may stretch out for years. Children often struggle with bio-parent loyalties. They may harbor anger or guilt. They may fear losing something that ties them to one or both bio-parents if a new person steps into the picture. In extreme cases a child may have been indoctrinated with a fabricated mythology regarding who the non-custodial parent is.

Even difficult behaviors can be opportunities to make progress if you are willing to adjust your perspective and see the moment from a different point of view. Blending a family means we are constantly learning. One of Leah's favorite how-to books is dog-eared and highlighted on almost every page. Its title tells the story—*How to Talk to Anyone about Anything*. It seems appropriate to share a quote that gave us new insight about how to deal with even the most difficult behaviors:

Anger is a plea for love. When people make bitter statements, they are sending the message that they need compassion, healing, and understanding. Just asking a simple, 'What makes you feel that way?' or 'What can I do to help?' immediately helps people feel calm and valued. Empathy and encouragement help difficult people transform! ...Your intention isn't to change people. It's to connect with them.

Healthy Blending

Children, even if they are adults, need to know their relationship is safe in spite of a new person's involvement in the family circle. A couple in this situation should do all they can to grow the collective relationship through healthy interaction, frequent activities, support of the children's interests, kindness, and respect.

Some of the children may be dealing with circumstances that are out of their control. One possible example is an aggressively negative, intimidating, or even abusive reaction by their other bio-parent against the developing circumstances. Our interactions with each of our children have always emphasized respect for their other bio-parent. It may be difficult, depending on your relationship with the former spouse or their behavior. However, it is a must if you want to give the child a fair shot at healthy development.

We have tried to send our children a clear message that we are safe to come to at any time with questions or struggles. We do this by actively listening not just to hear, but to understand. It is important to resist the temptation to immediately jump into judging and fixing mode. A couple in this situation can expect to field difficult questions. Some of the questions will not originate with the children but are fed to them by others. Sometimes it may feel like you are taking verbal body blows as children thrash about in their own lives trying to find a way through their emotional jungle. Give them time and space. You will hear their feelings. It will probably surprise you how basic concerns can morph over time.

One of our son's struggles came out in an unexpected way. He sat with Clark on a cold winter afternoon after spending time together and said, "How can I ever find a girl that will want to marry into our family?" Some discussion followed revealing this was not a statement about our marriage. It was more about how he was trying to deal with his own dynamics with stepsiblings, bio-parents, and siblings. He had struggled to reach a place where he could safely build a life. But he had serious doubts that anyone from outside the family could make the difficult journey. These were fair concerns. Clark's response not only comforted him but proved to be prophetic. "I promise that God is preparing a young lady for you. She will understand your complex family situation and be devoted to you."

It is not enough simply to refrain from defensive campaigning or negativity toward former spouses. Our role is also to encourage the child to pursue a healthy relationship with the other bio-parent. There may be serious disagreements with former spouses or even an absence of healthy or rational communication. But they remain part of the child and that relationship must be respected. If you want to have a healthy child, you absolutely must encourage them and support them in loving your former spouse. The child cannot be turned into a battleground or go-between. There are always exceptions based on the child's safety, a parent refusing to engage, disappearing, or certain legal circumstances. The relationship cannot be forced in these situations.

Seek to foster a normal life with the child's school, friends, and regular activities. There may be obstacles with their other bio-parent, but your relationship will be blessed if you do everything you can to facilitate *normal*. Your children will appreciate and respect your efforts. They will also have a healthier outlook toward their own lives and adjust more comfortably to the blended family.

If you are not the custodial parent, these issues can be magnified although the core challenge is unchanged. Leah was the custodial parent, and Clark was not, so they saw both sides of these issues. It comes down to trust and respect for each child and generous portions of patience. Clark's opportunities to work through issues with some of his bio-children were limited. Yet each of his children knew that a far-reaching principle was in place.

He shared with them an analogy that resonated. He explained that he was a bridge builder rather than a wall builder and that there was a bridge built just for them. He further related that he figuratively stood on the bridge with open arms. One day when they decide to step onto the bridge, he would ask no questions and require no explanations. We must be willing to welcome children back on their own timing and in their own way, then walk forward together. It is one of the hardest circumstances to endure. But when they reopen communications, it will be all the sweeter because it has been their choice.

Our shared values include strong foundational religious beliefs. Paramount among them is that Jesus' great sacrifice atoned not just for our sins but can heal our pain, sorrows, and a host of other emotional, spiritual, and physical injuries. We recognized this great saving grace when one of our formerly estranged children reached out to reconnect with our blended family. Regardless of the time that had passed since our former relations or the hurt or misunderstandings occurring in the interim, a miraculous healing process occurred when once again we find them in our embrace. All sense of time vanishes and a feeling of always having been together fills the soul. We believe this is one of the evidences of how the Lord's healing sacrifice works in our everyday lives. Not only can this smooth the sometimes-awkward reacquainting process, but it also provides the hope and faith necessary to patiently and lovingly endure other ongoing separations.

An important caveat is necessary here. The healing effect described above can be prevented or undone if parents fail to let go of perceived or real offenses or hold former behaviors over their returning children's heads. The joy associated with the described personal miracle can only be experienced in an atmosphere of complete unconditional forgiveness, acceptance, and love.

We realize every situation is different, but the foundational principle is to start immediately to include and engage to the extent possible. It is important to be sensitive as you discover where each child is and begin from there. Force will never build anything in a blended family or any other family. It only serves to reinforce the ugly stereotype that may have already been implanted by a negative former spouse, movies, stories, and media. Love unfeigned and inclusion are powerful forces in overcoming all obstacles.

The Delicate Balance

The delicate balance is managing your own growing relationship while developing a new foundation unique to each child.

Technically, this building starts from the moment you meet. That is how a couple should think about it even if it is not literally the case. However, there is a period during which the couple requires their own time and space to determine if there is indeed something they want to build upon. This means that Leah simply could not march a new guy through her home every time she went on a date.

On the other hand, it is self-defeating for the single parent to date until the relationship becomes strong and potentially lasting, then introduce the fiancé as the potential new mother or father or worse, announce that a *special friend* is moving in with his or her kids. The pendulum cannot be allowed to swing too far to either end of the spectrum.

Conversations with blended couples who have experienced relationship problems have a common thread. Many of the difficulties that eventually became insurmountable had their beginnings in the little things that either were, or were not, paid attention to prior to marriage.

This is especially true if you have a former spouse attempting to manipulate the child's feelings or playing the guilt or loyalty card. Leah engaged in regular and open communication with her children about her dating experiences and feelings as the situation warranted. She involved them in taking the picture for her online dating profile, allowed them to answer the door, and briefly visit with her date. Involving children too much or turning them into a confidant is not a wise choice for them emotionally. However, measured degrees of involvement are important so they can feel included.

Leah created an environment of teamwork and trust. This early inclusion helped them embrace the concept that their mom was dating. This opened the door for discussion about the possibility of remarriage and what that would mean for each child. Thus a positive momentum was created as the process continued toward the time when she would become involved in a serious relationship. The result was a cooperative environment where the children were encouraged to provide feedback on their feelings and impressions as they emotionally prepared themselves for the outcome.

Some may consider this an unreasonably high bar that restricts adult freedoms in relationship development. This can be a real issue, but a single adult with children is not the same as a single adult without children. If you have children, it absolutely does change things. Whether or not we wanted it in our relationship development, the bar was higher. Respecting this truth will save a blended family much strife down the road.

Once the relationship is in the open, the couple should do everything possible to allow natural growth for all. This must be a process rather than a series of sudden surprises that further disrupt the children's lives and emotions. Early during the courtship, Clark was invited to family dinner at Leah's home. We laughed, talked, prayed, and had a great time. We attended the children's activities and spent time in their lives rather than requiring them to always come into our lives.

Clark's children were older and, in some cases, dramatically affected by continuing loyalty demands. He took Leah on a road trip to Santa Barbara, CA where his oldest son and daughter-in-law were attending graduate school. They spent a couple of days with them and attended a USC football game together. They have never forgotten the memorable experience of meeting Leah for the first time. It was something we almost didn't do. It became a foundational treasured memory. The dynamics and feelings of older children are just as important to consider as they are with younger children.

Create Healthy Patterns

In our case the investment of time in, and attention to, our children created a pattern that has continued to enrich these relationships. Such involvement allowed friendships based on mutual respect to develop naturally. Relationships developed in this way produce enduring ties that can withstand the storms that will surely come. Another pleasant positive was that the children's concerns about threats to their bio-parent relationships were eased.

In addition to making an effort to enter your children's lives, do not hesitate to share with them the funny or heart-warming anecdotes from your own developing story. One of our most endearing dating stories has brought joy, wonder, and laughter to our children upon its telling and retelling over the years.

While we were driving from Utah to California for the visit referenced above, we discovered something interesting. A nine-plus hour drive each way was enlightening. Leah brought some healthy relationship books and CDs that promoted conversation as we got to know each other better.

One of the books we read back and forth, depending on who was driving, was *Chicken Soup for the Couple's Soul.* One of the chapters is titled, "The Fortune Cookie Prophecy." It related a story from the life of one of the authors. He described how he was more or less a confirmed bachelor in his mid-twenties with an ever-lengthening checklist to which the woman he would marry needed to measure up. He related that his friends had become concerned that he would never get married and were alarmed that he so quickly dismissed dates based on their not living up to specific listed requirements.

By the age of thirty-two he writes he had serious doubts about whether he would ever get married. Then it happened.

A friend told him he had opened a fortune cookie. The fortune said simply, "You will be married within a year." The friend then announced he was engaged. Just a few weeks later, the writer relates that he opened another fortune cookie after dinner at an Asian restaurant and was astounded to read, "You or a friend will be married within a year." He met a woman soon thereafter and was married within seven months.

We laughed and scoffed at the same time. It was entertaining reading but clearly impossible. Neither of us had ever seen a fortune cookie remotely like that. They usually say something that is generic or flattering but too non-specific to take seriously. By this time our relationship was well developed, and we had become quietly engaged. However, due to our complex family situations, there had been no official public announcement.

About a month later, we had a game night at the home of a long-time friend and his wife. We agreed to bring dinner and chose Chinese takeout. Following dinner the fortune cookies were passed around. Our little superstition is that for a fortune to be meaningful you have to choose the cookie yourself so we each did.

During dinner we had related the "The Fortune Cookie Prophecy" story. We laughed and agreed it had to be an urban legend. Clark opened his cookie first, read it, and his jaw dropped. Then he laughed out loud. Our hosts guessed immediately what he was reading and asked him to share it. He struggled to compose himself and in an overly serious voice read, "You will be married within a year." It was stunning.

However, it was Leah's fortune cookie that threw us into a side-splitting conniption. Before relating what her fortune said, it is important to understand that when we met, she was a struggling single parent with five children at home or back and forth with their bio-dad. She worked odd jobs to support the family and struggled with financial assistance. Her situation was extraordinarily difficult, but she nevertheless inspired her children by dealing effectively with her circumstances without losing hope.

With that said, her fortune can be placed in the proper context. She looked hard at the small strip of paper and read, "Your financial prospects will improve greatly in the near future." As you might imagine, it broke everyone up with laughter. We feel blessed and happy to say that both predictions have come true. We haven't seen an interesting fortune cookie since.

In conclusion, start as soon as you can to involve your children in the magic and wonder that is developing in your relationship. Do not hesitate, within reasonable age-appropriate limits, to share your own feelings openly. Trust that those who remain aloof will return and accept them unconditionally when they do. Find a way to include each child in the dating process, and they will become invested. Such an investment in each other will return tenfold. It is an important part of establishing a positive, inclusive, and sturdy family foundation. Our blended family has not needed to lean on that foundation every day, but there have been times when it was absolutely necessary and made all the difference.

CHAPTER IV

Principle #3: The Foundational Characteristic

Adaptability

The year we were married, five of our children had already entered the dating scene. Three more were rapidly approaching that sixteenth birthday when group dating becomes an option in our home. Children's emotions are complex to begin with, but dating adds graduate-level layers. Social pressures exploded into the blending process. We had to quickly reassess and unify guidelines that had been established as separate families.

Open communication was again a basic ingredient. We have always felt it a parental responsibility to ask for, and get, appropriate details about who our children hang out with. This is a pattern that had to be tactfully transferred to dating. Soundly established patterns of communication and openness are not difficult to continue as children mature. But it does not happen without making it a priority. However, even established patterns may need to be adapted as situations change.

When Clark's oldest son turned eighteen, he noticed a subtle change in their interactions. Respectful pushback trickled into their communication as he struggled with developing desires for independence. There was nothing negative; it just felt different. One evening he stood in his son's bedroom doorway and had roughly the following conversation.

"Everything okay?"

"Yep."

"You sure? Is there anything I can do or anything you want to talk about?"

"I'm fine."

"May I ask you a question?"

"Sure."

"I've noticed a change in how we have been interacting recently. You seem farther away sometimes."

No answer.

"I remember when I was your age. It was stressful thinking about moving out or going away to college. Everything I had known was changing. I became a little edgy and anxious. Does any of that sound familiar?"

"Kinda."

"Is it possible that you might be preparing yourself for being on your own? Or maybe you have a lot on your mind."

"I'm okay, really."

"You know I love you and have so appreciated you as a son and friend. I feel kind of awkward too."

"Why?"

"It's my first time going through this too. I've never had a kid turn eighteen before."

Shared smiles.

"Whatever the reason, I want you to know that I'd still like to find a way to be part of your life. So as your life changes, I hope we can work together to find a place for your dad in the new setup."

"Okay, Dad, we will. Don't worry."

This conversation is typical of most we have had with our sons. One-word responses, one syllable if possible. But the brevity of the response is not indicative of the depth of emotions. The thought, concern, and love are there too. Life comes at young people fast and can often be unforgiving with its ever-intensifying demands. No matter the age, your children will always appreciate an understanding parent. They will find a place for that parent in their lives if you allow it to happen naturally.

In the case above, our son opened up and it became a joint effort once he understood it was awkward for his parent also. He learned he was not alone. His realization that we were on the same team rather than him being on his parent's team impacted his behavior.

Our children know we will ask questions about friends and require parental contact information. It has rarely been a flashpoint because we are as predictable as the sun rising in the morning. Consistency works over time if children know it is standard operating procedure and not about lack of respect or trust.

Sometimes as a precursor to such questions, we announce that we are required to be a parent for a moment. We ask a few questions and get the answers we need. There may be associated conversations that grow out of the initial questions. Then, like the 1960s-era television show *The Outer Limits*, we return them to their regularly scheduled programming.

There are many reasons this information has proven helpful. It continues to be important in the smartphone era since batteries die, phones are intentionally or accidentally muted, misplaced, out of reach, turned off, or simply not checked, and, of course, unexpected stuff happens in life. For example, over the last few years we have had to get used to texting as primary initial communication. It is a mystery why our kids do not answer a phone call but at the same time will respond immediately to a text. In addition, it seems like nobody checks their voice mail anymore.

One of our sons was on a first date with a young lady whose accomplishments were intimidating. As a high school junior on a date with a senior, there was conflict between his anxiety and the desire to be independent. He could not believe she agreed to go out with him. Nevertheless, we had a good talk as the date night approached. He wanted the date to be perfect and over-thought everything.

We heard nothing until he called about 10:00 p.m. as the date should have been winding down. Our son sounded highly embarrassed. He informed us that they were stuck on the freeway with a flat tire. Likely story, right? We had a good chuckle, then Clark and another of our sons drove about twenty minutes to where they found him pulled safely to the side of the freeway. Another half hour and the job was done, allowing the date to continue. Surprisingly, he discovered that the unexpected problem spiced up the adventure of their date and made for a more memorable evening. However, we are not recommending this as a reasonable approach to making a date more interesting.

We were gratified that he would contact us in that difficult moment. It gave us an opportunity to demonstrate that we are always there for our children. It was also an effective teaching moment for the son who helped come to the rescue.

An Open Home

We have always encouraged our children to invite their friends over and do our best to adjust even with short notice. It's no problem to set an additional place for dinner or have a friend join us on a family outing or during home family time. When in our home, these friends are treated as if they are our own children. They may be asked to help set the table, do the dishes, or participate in other activities. Our children have generally chosen their friends wisely. But there are times when an invited friend needs a stable home environment. We try to take each person as they are and start from there.

Our youngest daughter mostly has friends with solid standards and good common sense. However, there have been a few troubled kids over the years to whom she has attempted to provide an example and direction. Our experience with these youth is that they mirror the statistics provided in chapter one. They tend to be from single-parent or struggling, blended families. The common thread with these youth is they live in homes where the parental influence is confusing, disengaged, or frequently absent. As a result, little direction is provided.

Almost without exception, they literally feast on an atmosphere of a safe, stable home where adults are willing to listen and are not absorbed in their own problems, lives, or distractions. They eagerly participate in our family activities. The concept of a nightly dinner where the family actually interacts is usually a new experience. It is shockingly sad that such simple interactions seem unusual to a large percentage of young people. But we find it both with at-risk teens as well as those who come from more traditional parental situations. We are frequently surprised to hear one of these friends comment that they rarely or never engage in family activities or dinners in their own home.

We live in a conservative, working-class community where farms are intermixed with commuter subdivisions. It would be considered neither poor nor well-to-do in America. It is a community where ample opportunities exist for a good education, low or no-cost activities, and social services. Yet there seems to be no shortage of at-risk children struggling to make their way without any meaningful parental influence. Because our children are in school, they come into contact with peers who have a wide variety of family circumstances. It is no surprise that they come home with questions. We have tried to cultivate an environment where open conversations can safely occur.

The Key Trait

We make ourselves available to discuss the wise and unwise choices their friends may have made. It leads to conversations about the traits they should be looking for to promote solid, stable friendships. Then the conversation will inevitably turn to the kind of traits they should look for in a date and ultimately a spouse. Early in our marriage one of our sons approached with an interesting question.

When this particular son began dating, he would arrive home typically between ten and midnight on a Friday or Saturday evening. We'd hear the garage door close and prepare for his entrance into the house. We knew he would knock on our bedroom door and want to talk. He would usually sit on the edge of the bed for between twenty and forty-five minutes. We were often tired and sometimes had already been asleep. But when one of our children invites us into their life, the answer is always yes. So we listened, asked questions, listened some more, gave advice, and provided input. It has always been an informative experience.

During one of these late-night chats, he asked what traits he should be looking for in a prospective wife and how he could identify them during the dating or hanging-out process. It was one of those times when you offer a quick silent prayer, search your memory banks for insight, and hope you can come up with something meaningful. We were not disappointed when a flash of pure inspiration came simultaneously to both our minds. We answered by asking our son a question. "What do *you* feel is the most important trait in determining whether a person would be a good husband or wife?" We looked at each other and smiled, knowing we were on the verge of a moment of shared discovery.

Our son paused and then thoughtfully responded by suggesting several characteristics. He included intelligence, academic success, physical beauty, being good with children, respectful of parents, faith, athletic prowess, religious conviction, being in tune with spiritual promptings, and others. We told him these were all reasonable answers. Then we shared with him our inspiration that these traits, and many others, are important, but there is one foundational characteristic upon which all others may be built. By this time we really had his attention. He asked what trait that would be. The answer was then and has ever since been, kindness.

We have learned in the crucible of family blending that kindness opens the door to nearly all other virtues and spiritual gifts. Other worthy traits, especially the spiritual ones, flow to a person with a truly kind disposition, heart, and attitude. Even if worldly success eludes your family, dealing with difficulties is usually more successful when built upon this foundation. However, if one is unkind it will more than likely lead to a host of dark and destructive paths. When kindness is not present, the void in the soul must be filled with something. Unfortunately, that void is all too often occupied by entitlement, victimization, bitterness, envy, selfishness, anger, or ultimately, hate.

Kindness, on the other hand, intertwines with unconditional love, gratitude, faith, patience, forgiveness, and understanding.

It promotes taking responsibility for our choices, respect for others, and a humility that allows us to learn from mistakes. It dampens anger, bitterness, and loud language in the home. It allows parents to more easily set aside offense and remain free of pettiness.

There will always be moments when thoughtless or careless acts occur, resulting in emotional injury or unintentional wounds. But when a kind disposition is the foundation of your relationship, injuries may be rehabilitated and wounds healed. This is possible through the balm of understanding aided by forgiveness and a humble, penitent spirit.

When kindness is secondary or absent, the relationship can become a competitive, score-keeping exercise. Every minor offense threatens to dredge up years of pent-up hostility. Each mistake carries the weight of every dispute ever experienced. In such an environment, the simplest relationship necessities may become elusive. Even if a couple stays together, their relationship can erode to the level of dysfunctional college roommates. Children are observant; they will absorb the examples provided. It will affect their own abilities to cope with life and make it more difficult for them to develop healthy relationships. More importantly, children absorb kind examples quickly, and those experiences are reinforced as they see them replayed regularly in the home.

Example vs. Words

Parents cannot effectively teach kindness without becoming living examples. This blesses the family but also raises the bar in a couple's relationship. Our children are all treated as our children. It doesn't matter the path they took to arrive within our family circle. We are all one family trying to do our best, and we need everyone's effort to be successful. The prefixes of *bio, step* or *half* simply are not relevant. We know they watch us. Children in a blended family are sensitive and sometimes anticipate a caste system. But in our family, we strive for something different. We want them to feel loved for who they are rather than how they arrived or what their last name happens to be.

Life reminds us regularly that we are imperfect travelers along a shared path. There have been moments when we could have done better. However, with time and consistent examples, the atmosphere of kindness slowly enveloped us all. This is when the real miracle began.

On one occasion, we experienced real satisfaction when two of our twenty-something sons invited their younger half-sister to hang out and have dinner. They were working, attending college, dating, and living their active social lives. There was no reason they would have been expected to take time to hang out with their teenage sister except that they are kind. Can you imagine how great she felt being out on the town with two handsome guys? She was beaming when they arrived home. The treasure of family life is most richly experienced when parents observe their children voluntarily passing on positive learned behaviors. There are few better payoffs.

On another occasion, one of our sons who is a pilot invited a struggling younger stepbrother to take an airplane ride with him. You might imagine how our younger son, who had never been in a small airplane before, reacted. He will never forget this kind act.

Win-Win Strategies

We live in a world where competition and passion are worshipped as goals in themselves. Clark has interviewed numerous prospective employees who had recently graduated from top universities or graduate schools. On one occasion, he was interviewing an MBA grad from a prestigious East Coast university. The interview went well until the subject of the interviewee's negotiating skills came up. He had taken a win-at-all-costs style negotiating class. The interviewee reported that he was not concerned about having difficulty in any negotiating situation. His stated strategy when entering a meeting was to immediately announce what school he had graduated from so others would be impressed and intimidated. This naïve young man firmly believed they would agree with whatever he proposed. Obviously, he had never actually tried his strategy.

Clark remembers having to compose himself to mask his surprise. He responded by explaining that he had negotiated with senior government officials and the highest-level officers in top companies all over the world. Never had anyone used the tactic. He explained that flashing an educational resume simply was not relevant. He commented that it would most likely be seen as an indication of insecurity and therefore most assuredly impact one's negotiating position negatively. The interviewee was speechless. He had not thought beyond the narrative fed to him in school. He had never considered what his reaction would be if the strategy didn't work.

Blended families naturally involve some of the toughest and most sensitive life negotiations. The business world teaches that there are three types of negotiation outcomes: *win-win*, *win-lose,* and *lose-lose.* Our careers, as well as family experiences, have taught us that there are really only two possible outcomes. A win-win outcome means that both sides get something important to them but usually also compromise on other points. However, the outcome is sufficient to allow both parties to feel good about the result. A win-lose is when one side feels like they got what they wanted while the other side believes they were taken advantage of in some way. They feel they have lost something valuable in the process for which they were undercompensated.

Often these outcomes are due to differences in overall negotiating strength. Situational strengths can be used to obtain advantage over the party in a weaker position through leverage, force, threat, or intimidation. Some will argue this is indicative of strong negotiating skills. They may even wear it as a badge of accomplishment. But these would do well to attempt to see past the short-term win to the ultimate goal of developing a long-term relationship.

The problem with individuals who are driven to win every situation is that they forget there will most probably be another time when the other side holds the cards. The other side will then use their strength to get back what they perceived to have previously lost. The result produces a win for them and a loss for the previous short-term winner. Thus any perceived short-term win will, with further involvement, likely turn into a loss. It is also important to note that a win at the cost of the relationship going forward is always a loss.

Our conclusion is that in the long-term, there are no win-lose negotiations. They all eventually turn into lose-lose. It means nothing to steamroll another party in a negotiation even if you get everything you want. The true test of one's negotiation and relationship skills is whether you can do business with the other party again.

Family lose-lose negotiations usually involve domination, manipulation, or efforts to exert superiority. This is lazy interaction. It is also anything but kind. True, it takes more energy to listen, understand, be patient, and seek an outcome that is reasonable. But it is worth the effort.

The foregoing discussion should not imply that children should always get what they want, endure no pain or consequences, or run the household. A win-win interaction can be found more often in respect, understanding, and communication rather than in agreement. For example, the need to discipline a child will test your negotiating and communication skills. Yet, punishment for sport or making it up on the spur of the moment is unlikely to teach a child an enduring lesson.

A conversation about appropriate consequences given the behavior may also be painful. But when completed and the consequence administered, there will also exist the light of understanding even if disagreement lingers. Children will have had the opportunity to help identify the appropriate consequence and take partial title to it. They will also know that it was meted out with love and kindness. This usually will facilitate respect and growth rather than anger, producing a long-term win-win.

Our experience in working toward win-win situations on a foundation of kindness and understanding usually results in the child arriving at the proper conclusion before we ever say it. This is the best outcome. The goal is to recognize a spiritual prompting or set of facts and self-correct. When this happens, we recognize the experience has been embedded in their souls, and they have taken a step toward repeating the positive process on their own.

Recently, we noticed our high school daughter beginning to dress a little more edgy than we felt was appropriate. Shorter shorts, slightly more revealing tops, etc., were becoming a source of increasing tension. A tone of rebelliousness began to creep into her conversation. She would announce that she had bought them with her own money or that it was hot weather or some other pop-culture rationalization. After several run-ins produced tense, unproductive conversations, we sought a more inspired approach.

We sat with her in a calm setting and discussed the Apostle Paul's counsel to the Corinthians regarding the ability to see more clearly as one grows older and wiser. We then compared it to a pamphlet in which there is a specific section covering "Dress and Appearance." We allowed her to reread this section and asked her questions about what she thought it meant. In less than ten minutes, she was preaching to us the importance of making improved choices. We had experienced a shared win-win negotiation, and she never realized it.

The Labeling Trap

The pages of online websites, social networks, and the news media seem daily to place before us a new prominent athlete, politician, or celebrity who embodies an angry entitlement attitude. Name-calling, crude statements, pettiness, and the justification for being a classless winner or childish loser seem common. The tendency of individuals to label anyone with a different or contrary opinion on a given subject as a hater, pho-bic, or an enemy is perhaps the most hateful, narrow-minded, lose-lose strategy of all. Further, it promotes among young peo-ple a dismissive shallowness that can inhibit their ability to learn from experience. Thus they struggle to gain perspective and bal-ance. It is in essence the definition of bigotry. Labeling is not open-minded; it is a lazy way of shutting down discussion and preventing understanding.

Current society seems to be satisfied with behavioral, class, race, and religious divisiveness. It has become the cheap, careless, and easy way to deal with others. The world is overly quick to label and dismiss rather than learn. Children cannot avoid becoming aware of such destructive examples. Without in-home countermeasures, such behavior takes on a mainstream acceptable look. It is often referred to as the *new reality* when it is not real at all. In the long-term these behaviors destroy lives, most notably the lives of those who employ them. It takes more than words to unify, heal, and overcome. It takes a desire to understand, hard work, dedication, and a firm belief that there is a higher purpose in doing so.

We believe there is a higher, more effective law. This win-win behavior is what the Biblical writer Paul referred to as charity or the pure kind of selfless love the Savior has for us all. He provided an excellent list of characteristics in his first epistle to the Corinthians. Paul reminded the Corinthian Christians that charity is willing to suffer long, is kind, does not envy, is not prideful, self-involved or selfish, is not easily provoked, thinks not evil of others, and bears, believes, hopes, and endures all things. He told them that such a combination of characteristics will never fail. It is a list worth seeking to incorporate in each life and each family regardless of personal religious views. He continues his advice with a warning to be patient because we only know in part and our sight will often be unclear. Paul closes the thought with a promise that one day we will see the complete picture just as God does now.

We have endeavored to maintain this win-win environment of civility and respect within our blended family. An underlying culture of kindness has made this possible. Any family can do the same if positive and uplifting examples are consistently followed by the parents. Few things emphasize this more than kindness in your dealings with each other and your children.

Regardless of one's personal belief system, it is true that applying the Apostle Paul's exhortation toward godly charity will make a daily difference as you swirl around in the family blender. Kindness is the key to opening the door to that room. It is a room in which we should all try to dwell.

CHAPTER V

Principle #4: Real Love

Real Love vs. Counterfeits

As children of the 1960s and 1970s, we appreciate a good Beatles song. One of their many endearing tunes is titled *Real Love.* It relates how an individual's perspective changes when they meet that special person. Of course, finding real love is more than just love at first sight, being enraptured, or having a crush. It can be instantaneous but more often grows with time. There are numerous types and degrees of love. What we refer to here embodies a depth and breadth of commitment not found in the watered-down, superficial interactions that today's society would seek to justify within the definition of love.

Our youth are assaulted with the word *love* as a justification for almost any type of behavior. Some are confusing, wasteful, and distracting, while others are truly destructive. The world allows many of these variations to masquerade as love, adding further confusion. Society would have our children believe that any behavior is justified if you can claim it is motivated by some loosely defined notion of love. The definition of love can vary greatly depending on the objective or agenda of those sending the message.

A number of years ago, a movie portrayed a man and a woman constantly attempting to kill each other. Somehow in the middle of this running fight, their attempt to commit mutual murder suddenly became aggressively affectionate culminating with implied intimacy. The message, intentional or not, seemed clear. The idea that physical or sexual abuse can be the basis of a positive, loving relationship is ridiculous. It is one of the numerous destructive narratives with which society seems to be spoon-fed.

It is important to teach the difference between real love and selfish me-oriented greed, lust, convenient justification, rationalized acting out, property-focused control, anger or abuse-motivated possession, or careless, absentee relationships. These are examples of the countless destructive behaviors that demonstrate the absence of real love. Yet they are rationalized by segments of society as appropriate, enlightened, or even desirable variations.

Our children are bombarded with these dangerous counterfeits in film, print, news, and real life. These examples are often accompanied by a narrative or theatrical conclusion that would make it seem as if such relationships are enlightened, noble, successful, happy, and enduring. It is simply not the case. The healthy, positive truth we are talking about is the kind of real love that constitutes a long-term, selfless commitment. It is love that endures while growing with shared experience. This is embodied in the concept of unconditional love.

What Nourishes

Unconditional love includes demonstrated trust, respect, and loving acts of kindness. It means selfishness cannot be part of who you or your family are. A blended family often has both the opportunity and challenge to exercise such love in a unique way.

Remarriage can present unexpected difficulties with a former spouse when children are involved. Sometimes a former spouse may harbor festering ill will or unfounded hope that he or she can get back together. On other occasions, a former spouse may harbor aggressive or negative feelings. When a remarriage is announced, such feelings can turn to bitter campaigning. Emotional and sometimes irrational demands of loyalty may be placed upon the children by both sides. These can make the transition to blended family life infinitely more complex.

Most blended families face at least some of these obstacles. Ours was no different. We faced a bumpy road early on with potentially divisive situations and statements. It is important to recognize that such difficulties arise more from insecurity, disappointment, guilt, or frustration than from meanness. We made a decision to do all we could to try to find a way to demonstrate to our former spouses that we were not a threat to their bio-child relationship. Of course, doing all you can does not mean there will be change. Sometimes the ill will continues regardless. But the effort will be recognized by your children. The burden can be lightened with time and patience. Extending love without conditions allows both children and parents to strengthen their bonds.

Our youngest daughter, Leah's bio-daughter, loves her bio-dad and has engaged in somewhat regular interaction with him. Like all relationships it has its up and down cycles. It is a situation that could, if allowed, lend itself to a wide range of competitive behaviors or negative talk. Its divisive head has occasionally been raised when discussing consequences for inappropriate behavior and potential discipline. Playing parents off each other can happen unconsciously or in passing with innocent-sounding comments. On other occasions, it can be overt, manipulative, and threatening.

We have made progress over the years by choosing not to be in competition with her bio-dad. Instead, we have taken the path of encouraging and supporting the relationship. This allows her to live a healthier mainstream life without emotional baggage or torn loyalties. As an added benefit, her confidence in us increased.

An opportunity presented itself years ago when our daughter began to complain that it was boring spending time with her bio-dad. She explained that he always took her to the same fast food restaurant and, "They never did anything fun." Clearly it was in her long-term interest to have better experiences. We prepared a list of fun activities they could do together and places they could visit. Leah shared it with her former spouse. His reaction was initially defensive. But we noticed over the next few months many of their activities were items that had been on the list.

Our daughter did not know for many years that these ideas came from us. Her bio-dad took title to them and they became his. That was not only okay with us but was the healthiest way for it to play out. We made the suggestions with no strings attached, or it would not have been unconditional love. The ongoing payback of this and other similar efforts to promote their quality time has been a stabilized relationship. The bonus with our daughter has been a minimum of playing-off and parental competition in our home.

Small Stuff

Clark is the stepdad to this particular daughter and has worked hard to reach that delicate balance between the firmness that goes along with being the custodial father and having fun. The fun that develops family relationships is usually found in small stuff. They have a private joke that plays out whenever he makes a meal or snack. Regardless of the type of food, our daughter wants to have some, not just a taste but a helping. They are at the point now where this is anticipated, and Clark usually makes extra. He is actually disappointed on those rare occasions when she does not ask.

However, she will usually walk into the kitchen, smile sheepishly, and ask if she can have some, knowing that he made extra. When a child asks to share his or her life with you, or if a parent has an opportunity to share with them in some way, do it!

It is the little things that build relationships and allow your bio- and stepchildren to realize how much you love them. We have a saying in our family: "We don't care what path our children took to be in our family. We know we were all meant to be together, and they are all our children without prefixes." Certainly, there are times when a child will play a bio-parent against a stepparent. Don't take the bait. This is when a patient, loving response reminds them how you really feel. More importantly, there are actions you can take to anticipate or diffuse these intense moments.

Several examples may be instructive here. One common challenge faced by blended families is dealing with innocent or unintentional offenses that are more a creature of habit than actually intended. For example, frequently we do something nice for one of our children or their family. It might be an unexpected visit, a note, call, or gift from both of us. Our children are thoughtful and will often send a thank-you note via social media or regular mail. Sometimes these notes address only the bio-parent rather than both. This is not a huge affront, but it is nice to be thought of. However, forgetting a stepsibling or step-parent is a particularly noticeable oversight because a blended couple works so hard to be inclusive.

We suggest three ideas by way of response. First, do not be offended and do not react or respond immediately. Give them the benefit of the doubt. It was probably a simple oversight based on already formed premarriage habits. Second, don't hide it from your spouse. Bring it into open discussion and decide what to do. Third, the bio-parent should have a tactful conversation with the son or daughter. Point out that the gift or act was from both. Encourage them to remember that in the future and help them decide what, if anything, they should do to acknowledge their gratitude to the stepparent.

Another opportunity to anticipate and diffuse came when our first grandchild was born. We were so excited. However, our daughter in this case has a mother and a stepmother. They were both first-time grandparents and the situation with the bio-grandmother was sensitive. Leah chose to take upon herself the nickname, Nana, by which the grandchildren would know her. This also felt natural because Nana has been a nickname on both sides of our family. It also served to avoid any future competition or misunderstandings that might have arisen with two maternal Grandmas. It stuck, and she is known as Nana to all our grandchildren. Besides, Leah is quick to point out with a smile that she doesn't feel old enough to be a Grandma anyway. To her, Nana sounds younger.

Clark has had to deal with an interesting challenge regarding our children's affection and loyalty. To appreciate this, it is important to note that of his four step-sons, his two youngest— one-and-a-half and three years of age respectively when Leah and their bio-father divorced—have not had their bio-father in the home for well over twenty years. Further, Clark has been their everyday father for the last fourteen. Their bio-dad passed away from complications due to a brain tumor in 2010. Prior to his passing, we had worked to develop a relationship of healthy communication as best we could.

We worked patiently to build the relationship amidst much early defensiveness. As confidence improved, our interactions became more pleasant. We finally achieved a friendly relationship with our sons' bio-parent. Toward the end of his life, he shared that he felt comforted letting go because he knew his sons were in a loving home with loving parents and would be all right. It was a tender message and a great honor to have arrived at that point. His passing was difficult on his four sons, and his memory remains an honored part of our blended family.

The Heart Has Infinite Capacity

There have been moments when Leah's bio-sons wax nostalgic with affection for their bio-dad. This is especially true when they are together. We are not perfect and must admit that we sometimes privately question the apparent depth of their feelings having been the parents that were always there for them. Nevertheless, these outpourings have been encouraged and supported. We have grown to understand that it is not mutually exclusive to our own relationship with them.

Perhaps it is asking too much for stepparents to completely eliminate passing twinges of envy or competitiveness. It is important to understand that a child's love is not a zero-sum game. When they express affection for a bio- or stepparent, it does not mean they have less for the other. We are confident in our children's love for us and are not threatened. This healthy point of view, if sincerely arrived at, will strengthen your relationship with each child.

When your children marry, this principle also applies. You will appreciate the fact that having chosen someone to marry does not diminish their feelings for you. It will in turn ease this important *second-degree* blending.

In extreme, but not uncommon, circumstances, the non-present bio-parent can be difficult to deal with—abusive or even toxic. Regardless of their behavior, it is possible that the bio-children may revere them and long for their association. Unless association is deemed dangerous to their well-being, it is important to do what you can to facilitate a relationship on some level, even if it is only possible within defined boundaries.

Sometimes the non-present bio-parent endeavors to drive wedges between the children and their custodial parents. This presents a challenge that can place stress on the marriage. Yet children are relatively quick to recognize the truth in their hearts. They may be unwilling to act on their feelings or unable to fully appreciate reality due to skewed loyalties, but they will eventually come around. By its very nature, the passage of time creates emotional space, which in turn promotes a clearer, objective understanding. This is where living a life of unconditional love and kindness will set your family apart from a home where angst, anger, and victimization dominate.

How has our family learned to deal calmly with such ongoing situations? It is because we have endeavored to understand the workings of the heart. It is also because we try to apply unconditional love in a culture of kindness. This exemplary type of love is what the Savior has for each of us. We must try to have it for others even if it is not reciprocated.

The heart is an amazing organ. You can love someone with all your heart. Amazingly, it does not prevent you from loving another in the same way. An individual can be the most important person in the world to you. Yet, the heart can still expand to include the same intensity of love for others.

We remember this with the births of our first children. How is it possible to love anyone as much as you do your first child? It is a life-changing miracle. Yet, when your second child is born, you feel the same way. Your love for them is also boundless. This will be repeated with all those who come into that special part of your life.

Of course, loving a second child so deeply and completely does not diminish the depth of love you have for your spouse or your first child. This is also true of blended families. Loving your stepchildren does not diminish in any way feelings for your bio-children. It is the miracle of the heart and soul's spiritual capacity for unconditional love. It can expand infinitely. It is this ability to intensely love others without detracting from those already loved that makes the heart phenomenal. In practice you must show your children you have such love for them. It is done by investing your time and attention in small and simple acts that tell them they are dear to you. No one else can do this for you.

A few years ago one of our twenty-something sons went through a period where he significantly reduced his involvement in our blended-family circle. The reasons behind such hesitancy are always complex. Loyalty conflicts with a bio-parent, a difficult job market, and a desire to be independent were all present. He had moved about forty miles away for work and was struggling in almost every aspect of life. His self-esteem and confidence were also at a low point, and the distance made it more acute. The most concerning aspect of this period was his unwillingness to accept help. It was nearly impossible and highly inappropriate for us to force the relationship at this point. Sometimes patience is the only arrow remaining in the quiver until life events create an opportunity to demonstrate unconditional love in a way your child will recognize. Then came one of those moments.

The unexpected opportunity came on a bitter-cold Sunday evening. It was one of the coldest nights of the winter with temperatures hovering below zero. The phone rang about 11:00 p.m. after a heavy storm that deposited close to a foot of fresh snow. Snowplows had worsened the situation by pushing the new snow to the side of the road where his car was parked. The relatively flat gutter in front of his apartment dropped to a one-foot-deep crevice just before entering a drainage culvert. The front wheel of his sedan had become wedged in the slot with the rest of the car embedded in an impressive plow-created snowbank. He had to work early the next morning, so the problem required an urgent solution.

Clark threw a couple of shovels in the 4x4 and drove the treacherous icy roads to his apartment. Twenty minutes of effort to get the car unstuck were fruitless. The icy hole allowed no traction. The front wheel drive tires simply spun and whined. They strategized about what to do. In desperation, they decided to visit a nearby all-night big box store and get several bags of salt and a cord of wood. Another forty minutes and a lot of shoveling later, the wheel finally gained traction on a path of wood and salt. The car was extracted just in time to avoid being reburied by the returning snowplow.

It is hard to imagine a less conducive environment for a father and son to build a relationship. But joint problem-solving in extreme circumstances can produce change. This was one of several tipping points that kept communication open during our son's most discouraging period. This and other similar events became turning points in our relationship with him. The openness we now enjoy has not eliminated all the rough patches. However, he now has a foundational understanding of our unconditional love and support. It will continue to make a tremendous difference.

We had an interesting and potentially volatile situation arise with one of our daughters during her teen years. We were out on a couple's date night for dinner and a movie. She was at home. We have strict rules about friends coming over without permission when we are not there. These extend to a complete prohibition of young men coming over when we are not at home. When the movie ended, we noticed our daughter had called. Leah called her as we drove home, and our daughter immediately confessed to having had a boy in the house. Apparently, the boy showed up unexpectedly to chat, and they talked at the door. She invited him in for about ten minutes, and they spoke in the entryway. She later related that she felt uncomfortable, ended the conversation, and the young man left.

We considered this a serious breach of our trust and poor decision-making on our daughter's part. We got the complete story from her upon our arrival home. It was tempting to lower the boom, but we held off. We discussed that it was a very serious situation and that we would let her know in the morning what we decided regarding consequences.

We sent her to bed and talked and prayed about what to do. Our dilemma was this. A serious breach had occurred, and consequences were appropriate. She knew this too. On the other hand, she had shown courage in immediately confessing, and we didn't want to discourage her from coming to us in the future. This is a common parental puzzle. Then we received the inspiration we sought.

The next morning, we met with her and expressed our concern about her judgment during the evening before. We explained that there was a serious need to rebuild our trust. We also put that particular friendship on probation and informed her that she would have to communicate with us in significant detail of any activities involving that individual in the future. The atmosphere was heavy with her anticipation of consequences when the kicker finally came.

We told her that although we were very concerned about her error in judgment, there would be no further consequences. She looked at us with relief but also with a confused, "Why?" in her eyes. Our answer was that there would be no further consequences because she was honest and immediately confessed her error.

We said, "While there are consequences for mistakes and poor behavior, there must also be positive consequences for making good and important decisions. Your decision to be completely honest was an important and very good decision."

This experience is etched in her mind because it both reinforced the value and importance of honesty in our relationship as well as the fact that we had real, unconditional love for her. This strengthened our relationship with her in inestimable ways. You might rightly assume she has not come close to such a situation again.

A Process Not an Event

Real love is not built in a day, nor is it spawned by a singular selfish, lustful act or longer-term casual, careless interaction. It grows with purposeful relationship experience and demonstrations over time. It tells someone that you really do love unconditionally. It is a work that takes regular nourishment. But it is also a joy that fills your life and family with real, enduring, I-am-always-there-for-you happiness.

One day when someone you have loved passes away—a spouse, a parent, a child, a close friend, or mentor—there will inevitably be an empty space that cannot be filled. It is okay if it remains unfilled or on hold, longing for the reunion that one day will surely occur and fill the space anew. The empty space is not a defect, because the heart continues always to increase and include others without limit. One should also note that it is not really an empty space; it is filled with fond and tender memories. This is real love. It is unconditional and will never fail. It is worth seeking and nurturing in your family.

CHAPTER VI

Principle #5: Bio-Compasses

Where Am I?

We both own compasses and have a rudimentary understanding of how they may be effectively used. The art of using a compass is fading into history due to the advent of global positioning satellites (GPS), smartphones, and other GPS-enabled devices. Yet an experienced outdoorsman carries a compass as a backup. The outdoorsman knows that a compass never has a dead battery or is out of its service area. The question is, "What basic functions do compasses and GPS devices perform?" They are quite different in their approach to answering similar questions.

Let's start with a GPS device. What does it tell you? Clark has asked that question in several presentations and usually gets answers like, "It tells you how to get somewhere." This is technically correct because many GPS devices have sophisticated map systems incorporated into their software, providing directions and much more. But this answer does not get to the heart of the modern GPS miracle. The core technology of a GPS system is that it can tell you not where you are going, but *where you are*. It does this with incredible precision. If a GPS system couldn't identify where you are, directions could not be provided to help you get anywhere else. It is the foundational data point upon which all GPS devices operate.

A compass, on the other hand, has a dial or arrow that points toward magnetic north. Unless disrupted by other magnetic fields, it will always reliably point in that direction. A compass is a tool that allows an individual with a map and knowledge of their location to work out how to arrive at any given destination. This is called orienteering. A compass cannot by itself tell you where you are, nor where you need to go. It also needs a known starting point. However, with a starting point, it will keep you on a straight path. The key to success with both devices is learning how they can be effectively used, what additional tools allow them to become useful, and, of course, practice.

The concepts of both these technologies have clear application in our lives. First, it is difficult or impossible to know how to get to a desired destination in life if you don't know where you are. In addition, once your journey begins, it is important to have a way to know when you are off the path. It is also important to know how to get back on track if you stray.

Children in blended families have often had their lives badly disrupted. Their internal compass can be disoriented. They may feel that a formerly clear, wide path has been obliterated by events they were helpless to avoid. You don't have to be a child in a blended family to experience this. Anyone who has moved to a new location for work or school understands to some degree.

Managing the Topography of Change

Our family loves to mountain bike. One of our favorite trails starts at the top of Bald Mountain in Sun Valley, Idaho. This narrow, single track runs along the ridge then off the backside, winding almost entirely around the mountain until eventually ending at the base of the Warm Springs ski lifts. We have ridden the trail several times and are familiar with its twists, turns, and beautiful views. Imagine our surprise a few years ago to discover a lightning storm had ignited a devastating wildfire burning thousands of acres including an extensive portion of the trail area. A beautiful forest was reduced to an endless stand of branchless, charcoal telephone poles. It was like traveling on a moonscape rather than in the forest we had grown to love. Nothing looked the same. The resulting terrain was unidentifiable. Fortunately, the trail was still visible, but the landscape was unnerving and disorienting.

As a previous chapter describes, divorce or death is dislocating enough. When compounded by remarriage and associated disruptions, children are left on a figurative moonscape. How can they reorient to where they are and who they are? Can their limited tools get them back on the path and refocused on previous goals? They are like the mountain biker or hiker lost in an unfamiliar forest.

Creating a new environment and building confidence takes time. During that high-risk reorientation period, straying even a few degrees can leave a child far off course. Some positive components should be immediately present. For example, on the surface a child may begin to thrive again in a home with a predictable schedule that includes school, activities, etc. But the structure needed to foster a healthy life goes far beyond having time filled with things to do.

There is an emotional reconstruction that needs to take place with the custodial bio and stepparents. Complexity is added because this must be done while transitioning to a healthy association with the noncustodial bio-parent. A foundation can be built through an environment of support, kindness, and unconditional love where communication and real listening occur on a regular basis. Quality time will also help. If new wounds are not regularly created, the initial disruptions can recede and emotional healing take place.

However, even during an ultimately successful reorienting process, there will be times when situations arise to challenge the developing structure. This is most common as new family rules and guidelines are established. Providing necessary, perhaps unwanted, advice and administering consequences for inappropriate behavior can also sidetrack the process. These are necessary steps and will promote a healthy home in the long-term, but they can also add discomfort. That is why it is important how parents manage the process.

Parents cannot default to dictating how things were done in the past. Neither can parents disengage or allow a particularly difficult child to commandeer the home. Recognize that the terrain and dynamics have completely changed. Parents must adjust to the new reality they have created and are continuing to create.

We have observed parents in some blended families who become hesitant to engage for fear of damaging their relationship with a particular child. This unhealthy alternative too easily defaults to abdicating the role of parent while attempting to become the child's friend or buddy. Of course, parents need to be friendly and kind to their children. This can be a basis for creating trust and confidence. But they are not merely friends, they must be parents too. Continuing to be engaged as a parent is an act of unconditional love.

Disengagement degrades the parent-child relationship and robs the child of important support and tools he or she needs to navigate. A disengaged parent forces a child to make their own choices without the benefit of critical adult perspective. It handicaps the child's ability to reorient. Even a healthy teen in a non-risk environment makes unwise choices. This goes with the turf and is why parents in general are critical to proper development. But a child in a disrupted, at-risk environment where parents are distracted and disengaged has the deck stacked against them. From a blended parent's perspective, abandoning them at such critical times out of fear, insecurity, and inability to cope or under the context that the child must *do their own thing* may be easier, but it is a selfish cop-out rather than love.

Stepping Out of the Shadows

One of our greatest delights is the process our children have gone through during their teenage years. Perhaps you are thinking this is when kids are the toughest. It can be a difficult time with all that is going on physically, emotionally, and socially. But there is something else amazing happening that no parent should miss. It is the miraculous process of a child stepping out of the shadow of their older siblings or parents to become their own person. Society begins to recognize them as an individual with a name, personal attributes, and unique achievements. Their identity begins a shift toward independence. Suddenly, they are no longer referred to as *the daughter of* or *the little brother of.* They spread their wings to develop their own passions and interests. This is a positive process, which should be celebrated and encouraged. Of course, they are not adults and should continue to have parental influence. But they need to be given enough space so they can successfully negotiate their test flights.

We have rules in our home for our children residing there, including adult children. Of course, some of these rules are modified as they mature. But we do not associate increasing privilege with age, we relate it to behavior. Turning sixteen does not mean a child in our home automatically drives or dates or has a later curfew. There is a process one goes through to get a driver's license. There is a process our children go through to receive advanced privileges and responsibility.

Driving involves classes, tests, periods of probation, and restricted driving with parents. When they begin to drive solo, they are limited to driving to and from specific, agreed-upon locations using familiar routes with no friends in the car. This provides relatively low-risk opportunities to practice until they have demonstrated sufficient judgment, common sense, discipline, awareness, respect for others, and a fuller appreciation of rules and laws. Demonstrated responsible behavior begins to create healthy habits. These in turn build our confidence and allow us to extend additional responsibility and privileges.

Our oldest son is a certified pilot and flight instructor. One of the more interesting aspects of this process was the requirement to learn instrument-only flight. While doing so, he wore special goggles that limited his sight to only the instrument panel. He found this non-intuitive at first. He realized just how dependent he was on his senses for information. He also learned how easily senses, equilibrium, and perspective can be fooled. The lifesaving truth is in the instruments. He has now arrived at the point where he is comfortable using instruments only. This served him well on one flight when the plane lost all communication, navigation, and electrical, including use of his flaps. Experience, calmness, and trust in his skills and instruments allowed his safe return, although he said a side-slip landing without flaps was a bit hairy.

Children are often presented with choices that may differ from family rules, shared religious beliefs, or wise, common-sense behavior—instruments that reliably define their lives. Some of these choices may in fact involve spiritually eroding alternatives. As our children develop their own structure and compass, we have chosen to give them gradually increasing responsibility. This includes the opportunity to accept the consequences that go with choices made. There cannot be much argument since they know the rules and consequences ahead of time.

With adult children, the dynamic does not change. Their behavior determines levels of trust rather than simply the fact they have celebrated their sixteenth, eighteenth, or twenty-first birthdays.

The Delicate Balance

There is a delicate balance in transitioning from strict rules to consent, communication, and choice. It occurs over several years. However, regardless of age, there are two things we feel is always our responsibility to make sure our children understand. First, we feel it is our duty to make sure they know exactly how we feel about the situation, and why we feel that way. This must be conveyed prior to making their own choices, especially if there are questionable alternatives. Such sharing must be done sensitively and with respect, or it can easily become manipulative. Second, it is important to discuss what we understand God has said on the subject since in our family this is a critical foundational belief system. The latter perspective is important because as parents we believe that it is our responsibility to reinforce God's teachings. It is part of the process of helping them to understand why they are important to us and how obedience can bring true happiness. Then, depending on the level of demonstrated responsibility, we turn the decision over to them.

We have found this process to be most effective when they get the result first and then discuss the issue at hand. It might include stating at the beginning of the conversation, "You are not in trouble" or "We are not mad at you" or "We believe this is an area where you are capable of making your own decision." This promotes listening and understanding during the conversation because they no longer are distracted by where it may be going. Anticipating when the next shoe will drop can easily sidetrack communication. This approach also opens the door to better absorption of the counsel and perspective they may need to make the best decision.

One example is the type of music mixes youth have available on sites like iHeartRadio or Pandora. Anyone with internet access can tune into a genre. Keep in mind that the breadth of any specific genre is decided by someone else. Therefore, these can include questionable music mixed with acceptable tunes. Our advice has been that it is not enough to simply look at the genre or lyrics and determine they are acceptable. The question we ask them to consider is whether the music is uplifting or contributes to positive and happy feelings. Getting them in touch with their own feelings and spiritual insights gives them valuable tools they can use in society.

Teens especially tend to focus on end points: right or wrong and good or bad. Parents contribute to this if they simply focus on the black-and-white of situations. But maturity comes as they are better able to discern trends that nudge them toward or away from the end points. Learning to identify what is uplifting or promotes positive thinking are critical skills often overlooked in parenting. It is not enough that your child is staying out of trouble. He or she must be going somewhere better. This is always found in the small stuff.

For instance, we shared our thoughts and spiritual insights on a particular subject with one of our sons who was in the throes of making what he felt was a particularly difficult peer-driven choice. Should he go with his friends to a popular but questionably rated movie? We discussed the reviews and possible reasons for the rating. At the end of the conversation he said, "It would be a lot easier if you would just tell me what to do." He said it with a smile, but we all understood the message. Taking responsibility can be a burden, but it also empowers and drives healthy development.

It may be simpler in the short-term to be a parent or a child when decisions are dictated. But it is harder to take ownership of the decision or learn from resulting consequences. It is empowering for a teen to tell their friends that they choose not to attend a particular movie because they personally do not feel good about it. It is ineffective and squirrelly to say, "My parents won't let me." Certainly there are times when parents must say no to protect or allow survival. But real growth happens when children feel part of, and responsible for, their choices.

Growing Up is Messy

An important aspect of children taking ownership of their choices is allowing them to problem solve. This often runs counter to the strong feelings for each of our children. As such we must resist our first impulse to give the correct answer, fix the problem, take the heat, and prevent them from the pain, injury, or consequences of their mistakes. We don't want to see them hurt and would, without hesitation, take their place if allowed.

Unfortunately, life doesn't usually work like that, and it is unwise in the long-term anyway. It has been extraordinarily satisfying to watch our children grapple with the challenges of life. They grow, mature, and figure most things out. This doesn't mean we refuse to help. We are always there for them. But it does not help if we do it for them. In many cases, it is impossible to step into their shoes. Parents who are always intervening simply shove their children out of the driver's seat and sometimes out of the car altogether. It makes it hard to develop confidence and even harder to deal with the next challenge.

One of our twenty-something sons ended a several-months-long dating relationship. It was a traumatic struggle but a wise decision. However, it involved loss of time in college and the cost of an engagement ring, which he had paid for out of his own earnings. It was an expensive lesson. Our children understand that lessons learned in the school of life often require a tuition payment. Life's tuition payments are usually levied in emotional, spiritual, or physical terms. In this case there was also a real financial cost. Successful problem-solving skills are best developed by experience, with a dash of well-timed advice.

Another one of our college-age sons worked for many months to gain entrance to one of the most selective and sought-after educational departments on campus. The competition was extreme and the coursework demanding. We were pleased to discover he had been accepted. He learned much by persevering and problem-solving to overcome the numerous obstacles.

However, after a semester in the program, he decided it wasn't something he wanted to pursue for various well-conceived reasons. He made the difficult emotional decision to change departments. There was disappointment because he felt he had given up. It was true that he had worked hard to gain acceptance. But changing course is not giving up. It happens as we learn. Several months later he was enjoying his newly chosen field of study and has not looked back.

The Bio-Compass

There is a unique twist in this principle that is common in a blended family. In some of the circumstances discussed, there may be moments when the bio-parent is the only one who can deal with a situation. The stepparent may be capable, but ineffective, in giving the same direction. It is important for parents to recognize such situations and avoid falling into the "I'm the dad or mom so do what I say" trap. The answer inevitably will be thrown back in your face. "You're not my dad (or mom)!" Voila! A new dispute has suddenly arisen that has nothing to do with the interrupted discussion. Even more dangerous is the, "As long as you live in my house…" approach. A parent should beware of ever using such threats without thinking of the most likely, "Then I'll leave…" response.

Trying to force something is never an effective way to parent and is a particularly destructive strategy in a blended family. Therefore, it is important to acknowledge that there are times when the bio-parent can more effectively deliver a tough message or sensitive but needed advice.

This plays out in countless ways. It does not diminish as children grow older, enter their twenties or thirties, move out, have their own lives, or get married. You will never cease being a parent. They will come to you with a variety of financial, employment, dating, child-rearing, and marriage challenges or questions. There will also be times when a child will come to the stepparent with such queries rather than the bio-parent. This is usually because they recognize particular experience or insight. Sometimes they will not readily open up about their struggle. Reach out to them and patiently inquire. A phone conversation with one of our college-age children started like this:

"Is there something we need to talk about?" We knew there was, of course.

"Yes," came the answer.

"Name the place and time, and we'll pay for what we eat while we talk," was our response. Breakfast or lunch is a great investment in keeping the lines of communication open.

It is natural and right that a blended couple should desire to visit with a child together. But that is not always possible or advisable. When only one of the parents is involved, they should communicate the conversation with their spouse and seek additional guidance. The parent not consulted must set aside any pride or perceived offense. Find comfort in the fact that the child has sought out parental advice. This is yet another reason why it is important that all parents, especially blended-family parents, are on the same page. The parents must absolutely trust each other and have confidence in each other's ability to provide the necessary guidance or seek additional insight. The key is to lovingly defer, if necessary, to the bio-parent and not allow pride to interfere.

This has been particularly true with our girls who seem to have a more developed bio-compass than our boys. For example, tone of voice may be an area that your daughters are particularly sensitive to. We have found this to be particularly true in our family. This may differ with other families, and the degree of difference certainly varies with each of our children, but it is generally as stated.

Bedtime, homework priorities, appropriate school dress, curfews, pets, and appropriate friends and activities are common flash points. In addition, teens have the additional complication of chemical and hormonal changes. This can make such flash points more unpredictable. It is important to enter these minefields carefully and together with a unified, well-discussed general plan.

Roles and Teamwork

Both parents may be present when the conversation ventures into one of these bio-compass areas. It takes courage and maturity to step back and hold your tongue when your spouse is responding to the situation. This doesn't mean one checks out, rather it means you support and act as a resource. There will be opportunities to participate in a supporting-cast role. Your children will see trust, love, and mutual support in action while you work through the issue. This will help them employ healthier patterns of dealing with stressful situations in their own lives. Another positive result is that children's trust and confidence with the stepparent will be enhanced. It will inevitably lead to their compass pointing to both parents more equally.

What do parents do when advice cannot be given in person? When a child comes to the bio-parent in the form of a phone call, there are always two choices. First, the phone can be placed on speaker so both parents can be involved in real time. However, this is not always the best approach unless you first obtain the child's permission.

If only one parent is on the phone, the other parent should not try to make comments or toss out distracting ideas. It interrupts the call by making the parent on the phone listen to two conversations at the same time. Certainly, the non-involved parent should be available if an answer or advice is necessary. But trying to intercede will only hamper the ongoing communication and irritate the parent on the call. Be patient; the time will come.

Another important warning about dealing with the bio-compass is when you are *in the moment.* This refers to trying to force working through the problem when your child is in the midst of his or her emotional whirlwind. Listen, understand, and look for a calmer moment when the child can focus. Leah is especially skilled at this, while Clark occasionally tends to be a bit of a bull in a china shop. There are times when the roles reverse, but generally, Leah treads more lightly.

In the middle of writing this chapter, we received a call from a distraught teen. A teacher confiscated her phone for the rest of the school day. Apparently, she was using it during class to make plans for lunch and after school. Certainly a no-no but also a bit ticky-tack since it is a rarely enforced class rule. We knew there was more to the story, but Leah listened as our daughter vented, then offered a few suggestions. Feelings calmed. It turned out not to be the end of the world after all. She realized she might just make it through school without her phone. Small issues like this may be traumatic in the moment but don't require children to be fixed or saved. Rather, a listening ear and understanding heart is sufficient. The teaching moment can come later when emotions have calmed.

However, we have observed some family reactions where even this kind of a small situation boils over into arguments and hard feelings that last for days. Old wounds are reopened, raising responsibility and trust questions that threaten relationships. Or worse, parents prevent the child from learning by problem-solving. Parents do this by turning on the school and teacher sometimes even escalating the matter to the administration.

Counseling Adult Children

Teenage issues can be challenging. But these are also training for the bigger trials that come later. All but one of our children are now in their twenties and thirties. Seven are married and four of these have children. This means we have additional parenting challenges not experienced with teenage children. There is a time in teenage lives that the great crises of the day involve not making a team, not being asked to the prom or being asked by the wrong person, mean kids, test stress, misunderstandings with teachers, or forgotten assignments. This is not to say that teens do not have serious difficulties in their lives or that those referenced do not loom large at the time.

However, it illustrates that many teens do not have the same perspective regarding the nature of the bigger challenges. By the time children get into their twenties, they begin to experience profound challenges like choosing a spouse, medical complications with pregnancy, graduation and career choices and disappointments, or losing a job for the first time. They may be faced with the realities of marriage and getting along with a spouse, caring for handicapped children, or discipline problems.

This is when a parent may receive a call at two in the morning and hear the dreaded, "I can't do this anymore," statement. Parenting then happens by consent and invitation, rather than position or title. This is the payoff for years of being there. These moments may be extraordinarily challenging. However, the experience can also be sweet, bringing families closer together.

But they are only possible because of long-term relationship development.

Some of the stories in these areas are too personal to relate. However, one common example is illustrative of the situation. One of our sons while in the dating phase of his life would contact us with some regularity regarding girls he was dating. A common question involved whether he should go to the next step of dating exclusively, breaking up, or getting engaged. He was like most young twenty-somethings. He wanted guidance and independence at the same time.

There were times in this process that he had conversations with both of us seeking our differing insights and perspectives. On the other hand, there were times when he was much more responsive to suggestions from his bio-parent. On one occasion, when he had been exclusively dating a nice young lady for several months, he regularly came to both of us. Suddenly, when the tipping point arrived, he sought his bio-parent.

He explained that he felt they loved each other and had dated long enough (about eight months). But he didn't have growing feelings for her. He expressed that because of the time invested, he felt it necessary to take the next step to get engaged. We had felt for some time that they did not have the required level of commitment to each other for marriage. They seemed to have more of a going-through-the-motions relationship based on habit and convenience rather than real love. However, we were committed to accept the young lady into our family and love her with all our hearts regardless of our reservations. The bio-parent shared these thoughts with him and he listened.

He is a thoughtful individual and considered the advice, but we heard nothing for several weeks. Then he called and announced that they had called off their relationship. He took ownership of the decision himself but was not uncomfortable seeking advice. We were happy to be a resource. It made no difference to us which one was the conduit.

Blended families must simultaneously pursue two paths. They must create a stable environment and provide the tools for each child to understand where they are, who they are, and where they can go from here. This is the most effective way to successfully reorient their bio-compasses. They must also be a flexible team so that children may safely seek guidance from either or both without offense.

In connection with this, any counsel provided must be given such that children have an opportunity to make the final decision. Only then can they learn from resulting blessings or consequences. Parents in a blended family will always ride the rollercoaster. But they also, by applying these principles, will have ample opportunity to stand back and watch the miracles and growth happen. Just remember not to stand too far off; you may be called upon at any moment.

Chapter VII

Principle #6: Time Travel

Quality Time

Several popular movies have dealt with the concept of time loops or time travel. *Groundhog Day* is one of our favorites. It follows fictional Pittsburgh TV Weatherman Phil Connors, an arrogant, self-centered personality, who finds himself trapped in a time loop, repeating the same day over and over. Various estimates have placed his time caught in the loop at between ten and fifty years.

His personality evolves as the character passes through behavioral phases. He experiences confused disorientation, selfish diversion, hopeless desperation, and personal betterment. Finally, he discovers generosity, virtue, and selfless compassion, which allow the time loop to end. The story and performances make it an endearing, enjoyable classic.

This fictional tale is impossible, right? We cannot repeat the same day over again. Don't be too sure! Some days seem like we've been there before. We are not, of course, talking about getting stuck in literal time loops. But individuals can repeat behaviors which result in similar experiences recurring on a regular or even daily basis. Most of us have had these cycles in our lives. The positive cycles raise us and our families up while the negative ones must be broken lest they become a downward spiral.

In the 1980s a pop-culture phenomenon arose. It was embodied in the phrase *quality time.* During this period a vocal cultural segment aggressively devalued stay-at-home parents. This demeaning focus was directed particularly at mothers who did not work outside the home, but it also affected fathers. It functioned as an extension of a covetous society flooded with social pressure to keep up in job advancement, power, salary, possessions, etc. This intense distraction damaged countless families.

There are legitimate reasons that two-income families are necessary. In addition, the single parent can also be unavoidably forced into the job market. We are not saying that this phenomenon always creates problems in families. However, it does result in additional demands and reduces the margin of error in raising children. In fact, we have seen instances of strong families and healthy parent-child relationships in single-parent and two-income homes. It requires a high level of organization and commitment but can be done. The point here is to address a justification concept born of a movement that created self-doubt in those who chose not to pursue their stated pop-culture values. It is not to evaluate the rightness or advisability of various family circumstances.

In the 1980s Clark was working in Los Angeles, fresh out of graduate school while Leah lived in Idaho, the Chicago area, and Arizona during the decade. The concept of quality time was a frequent topic of workplace and social discussions.

Parents working in the city would frequently be heavily engaged in developing professional careers and working long hours, including extended commuting and business trips. This meant their children would spend most of each day under the care of others.

There was at the time a subtle guilt that lurked just below the surface of the white-collar professional. Whenever the topic of children arose, it turned quickly to the quality time these working moms and dads had planned with their children on the weekend. They intended to go to the beach, the zoo, the park, visit family, or watch an athletic event together. Occasionally, a parent revealed they planned to have a long-anticipated conversation with a child on some point of discipline or development. Such involvement constitutes an important aspect of building positive family relations. Planning is critical or it likely will not happen. Yet a disturbing pattern was all too often apparent. These professionals began to be replaced in their parenting role by other daily caregivers, and parental influence waned in the home.

Their role evolved into that of a grandparent who visits on weekends, does a couple of special events with the children, and has a loving bond. But in general, the parental relationship slipped because they were not present on a regular basis. Grandparents can be a vital influence in a child's life, but not at the expense of having parents. Many of these upwardly mobile couples began to have discipline and acting-out problems with their children. The conversations turned from plans for quality time and lip service regarding how much they loved their children to concern that their children were spinning out of control.

This principle must be committed to by both blended parents. Sometimes this requires a change in jobs or hobbies for one or both parents. We recently noticed a frustrated post on a blended family-oriented Facebook page that unfortunately is much more common than one would hope to see. The mother was venting that her boyfriend with whom she was living regularly left for distant work that kept him away for days. She was left to single parent their blended family of five young children and at the same time run a preschool in her home. At the end of her tether, she was seriously considering ending their relationship even though she had strong feelings for her boyfriend.

Two problems seem to jump out of this developing train-wreck scenario. First, they both have different levels of commitment about successfully blending the family. This often happens when stronger plans and commitments are not made from the beginning. Second, one of the parents in this case does not get the concept of quantity time.

Quantity Time

The true principle slowly began to break through the pop-culture trend. The truth is that quality time cannot be neatly planned or scheduled. Quality time happens randomly. It is based on when a child needs the parent. That can happen at any time of the day or night. Our children need us when they need us. If we are not there, the role is filled by someone else, or not at all. Not having a parent present when needed has predictable short- and long-term consequences.

Gradually, some coworkers began to seek more time with their children. This involved changing their schedules. Adjustments included reduced hours, shortened commutes, working part-time, working from home, or becoming full-time, in-home parents.

Others, unfortunately, grew increasingly distant from their children. Their children became involved in distracting or destructive activities and groups. Too late, these parents discovered the truth of the statement spoken by nineteenth century writer and philosopher Elbert G. Hubbard:

No matter what you've done for yourself or for humanity,
if you can't look back on having given love and attention
to your own family, what have you really accomplished?

The concept of quality time still exists in society today. But its definition has changed to acknowledge that quality time cannot happen unless there is also a strong dose of quantity time. In our family we have found that both random and planned experiences are critical to healthy blended-family relationships. However, it is often the smallest, briefest random experiences that mean the most.

On a spring afternoon, we received a random call from a teenage daughter. It was the last day of the high school spring term, and she had a lot going on. She called on Leah's phone to tell us that her last final had just ended, and she aced the test. A brief, joyful interaction followed. It was a blessing to have her call. She was also uplifted because when she called, her mom was there to answer. They had one of those bonding in-the-moment conversations that would not have been the same several hours later. It was quality time. Later, when she walked in the door, the discussion immediately returned to her success of the day, and her parents were there to celebrate with her. Quality time is always enhanced by a shared experience. It was a perfect example of what cultural historian Catherine M. Wallace meant when she said:

> *Listen earnestly to anything your children want to tell you, no matter what. If you don't listen eagerly to the little stuff when they are little, they won't tell you the big stuff when they are big, because to them all of it has always been big stuff.*

Years later, the high school daughter probably doesn't even remember that particular moment, because in the grand scheme of things, it was small stuff. However, at the time it meant everything to her, and its meaning was magnified because it was shared with those she loves. Quantity time provides the opportunity to create such bonding moments.

Family Traditions Create Bonds

The need for family and individual time cannot be overemphasized. We have always had children with active, involved lives outside the home. Our approach has been three-fold. First, we proactively counsel with our children as they grow through the teenage years to help them choose extracurricular activities in moderation. It is good for children to be involved in music, drama, sports, community, and church service or the arts. Every child benefits by finding an appropriate activity during those challenging preteen and teenage years that they can use to develop their talents and self-confidence.

Second, our children know they can't be involved in everything, so choices are necessary to avoid over-programming. Our blended family rule is to try to keep such involvement to one primary activity if it is time-consuming. This has allowed them to excel and grow without unnecessary overload.

Third, we have a regular daily and weekly schedule of family involvement. This includes daily Scripture study and prayer, attending church services together and related involvement, a regularly scheduled evening during the week where family activities and learning occurs, and daily family meals. We do this in addition to the usual family-related outings, support of children in their activities, vacations, and holidays. This regular structure has been in existence from the beginning of our marriage. It has become an expected and mostly planned pattern of life for our children. There have been times when one or more members of the family have missed an event due to a legitimate conflict. But the closeness developed by this consistent pattern of quantity family time has also produced quality interaction.

Quality time that grows out of quantity time and family scheduling takes forethought. Being there when your children need you cannot be haphazardly pursued, or it won't happen. Grace Kelly, Academy Award winning actress and later Princess of Monaco, was quoted in a 1970-era interview with Family Circle Magazine on how she and her husband, Prince Rainier III, addressed the challenge of making time with busy schedules:

I am like anyone else trying to keep a home together.
I must fight, I mean fight, for the time to be with my
children. My husband and I spend every spare moment
we have with our children in an effort to share our lives
with them. And where there are no spare moments,
I struggle to make them.

It comes down to actual priorities rather than lip service. If children are a high priority, quality time happens. If not, parents miss these critical moments. Miss enough moments, and you erode and risk abdicating your role of mother and father. Others take your place, even though you retain the responsibility and biological title of parent.

If this can be categorized as an investment, then the return certainly comes along the way. But the best surprise comes after your children move out and then return for various events or to just hang out. This plays out with our adult children in the form of having lunch or dinner get-togethers as schedules permit. One evening we got a call from a twenty-something son who wanted to come over to play a popular card game. We think he chose the particular game because he usually wins. During our time together, he opened up about school, work, and dating. It was a perfect example of how unplanned quality time can occur with adult children.

One of our daughters-in-laws expressed her feelings about quality time during a recent visit. She confided that she and our son view visits to our home like a pilgrimage that rejuvenates them because of the positive spirit and atmosphere they feel. Another twenty-something son, when asked about what he might like for his birthday, responded that he would like to spend time with us doing something together. There are few more satisfying compliments that parents can receive.

Children benefit greatly from having structure in their lives. They need to have an environment that is stable, dependable, and safe that they can return to after their travels in an often unforgiving and tumultuous world. The quantity family experiences structured into our daily lives allow random quality moments to occur with regularity. We also encourage our children to participate even if they have friends over. This creates fulfilling opportunities for our children to impact the lives of their friends. Our dinners and family times always have room for a couple of unexpected guests.

It is important to note that sometimes turning quantity into quality takes a conscious effort. We frequently will take a son or daughter to breakfast or lunch with an agenda. We want to discuss how things are going, address a concern, or celebrate a success. Reaching out to initiate such events does not take formal planning. However, it does require flexibility to fit into their work or school schedule. But it is always worth it.

Our efforts to promote family time have not been without their bumps. We have a son that lived with us well into his twenties. He struggled with school, work, and social involvement. He pushed away for a time from religious and family activities and tended to isolate from the rest of the family. We tried everything we could think of. In the end the best approach was not to guilt him into or demand his participation. Rather, we let him know he was always welcome and extended invitations to participate. He always knew when we were having dinner or other family activities. Over time we added to that financial responsibilities, jobs, and his ability within an agreement to exercise his right to choose with clearly outlined consequences for positive and negative choices.

It didn't take long before he was participating regularly. He responded to a consistent, loving, outreached hand and made his own choice to participate. He ultimately went back to school and took some valuable steps forward. His journey is long from over. But as parents in a blended family, we have learned to celebrate progress whenever it happens. Small steps can one day become life changes.

Family Dinners

Space does not allow us to do a deep dive into the benefits we have seen from every type of family activity, so we will focus here on one in particular—family dinners. Both of us grew up having regular family dinners, so we appreciated their importance. It's a toss-up which they enjoy more—the positive and healthy interaction that occurs or Leah's gift with designer dinners. Conversations over dinner often include the suggestion that when she opens a restaurant, a particular meal must be included on the menu.

It might be easy to dismiss this practice as an archaic tradition of a bygone era. Certainly, today's society moves at a faster and more frenetic pace. With over-programmed schedules, two-salary families, and fast-food, one might be justified in asking whether family dinners deserve attention. Yet we have discovered that the simplest behaviors can have the most powerful effects.

There have been numerous studies that reveal the positive impact of families having dinner together on a regular basis. The sources are diverse, but the findings have a common thread. It makes a significant difference.

CNN reported on a 2011 Columbia University study that identified eight benefits for family dinners. USA Today in 2013 referenced research published in the *Journal of Adolescent Health* that confirmed a marked improvement in a youth's emotional and behavioral problems with each family dinner held. Both studies stated that, in the 11- to 15-year-olds studied, family dinners increased emotional well-being; trusting, helpful behaviors toward others; and higher life satisfaction regardless of gender, age, or family economics. The most stunning finding was that the effect was nearly immediate and almost always far-reaching. WebMD provides a summary of the wide-ranging benefits that accrue to families who spend an hour at the dinner table together on a regular basis. Regular in this case was concluded to be an average of five times per week.

1. Everyone eats healthier meals, including more fruits and vegetables.
2. Children are less likely to become overweight or obese.
3. Children are more likely to stay away from tobacco, alcohol, marijuana, hard and prescription drugs.
4. School grades are higher.
5. Children are willing to talk more and share feelings, especially related to serious problems.
6. Self-esteem is increased as children indicate they feel parents are proud of them.
7. Stress and tension are reduced in the home.

What family wouldn't benefit from these improvements? The referenced study recommends that even two family dinners a week would move the family dramatically in the described direction. It further suggests that extensive homemade dinners are not the key and that something as simple as order-in pizza also qualifies as a family dinner. Although pizza every night may not help as much with items one and two above. Regardless, the advice is to try to start with twice a week, keep it simple, emphasize healthy-meal alternatives, get the family involved in the preparation, make the discussions enjoyable, and create a relaxing environment with soothing music, flowers, or a candle. The real point is to sit down together.

One additional aspect is important to note before moving on. A family is not a herd of cattle grazing at random times. Too many families graze in the kitchen at intervals when hungry throughout the day. Passing each other during random grazing is not a family dinner.

There are countless ideas once you allow your creative juices to flow. Our family life can be hectic, so we have a roughly set time for dinner every evening around 6:00 p.m. It is flexible, depending on schedules, and sometimes we have activities that intervene, so it is not every night. But it is usually five plus nights a week. It is so engrained at this point that we frequently will get calls from one or more of our married children asking what we're having for dinner with the idea that they may join us.

Leah enjoys regularly adding her homemade touches to dinner, and the entire family is enriched by the effort. However, modern demands require us to work smart, so we often utilize the Crock-Pot to prepare simple meals. Putting dinner in the Crock-Pot in the morning eases the preparation and cooking time. It also makes the house smell fantastic when the kids walk in from school or other activities. The smell of a great meal does more than anything else to sell family dinner time. The problem becomes keeping everyone from early and frequent taste testing.

We also have developed several rules that make dinner time more pleasant. The dinner table is a *no phone zone*. Family members and visitors are invited to keep their phones pocketed or they may choose to place their phone in a basket on the counter. There are, of course, the occasional important calls that interrupt, and flexibility is key in such cases. However, most of the things we do on our smartphones are neither urgent nor important. Facebook, Instagram, Snapchat, YouTube, texting, selfies, downloading and experimenting with new apps, streaming movies or television, Twitter, gaming, surfing, and checking various media sites can wait.

In addition, we emphasize proper table manners during family dinners. We use it as a time when we can discuss how it prepares us for dating and life. Our children are instructed in being courteous and thoughtful during dinner. This regularly involves the terms *please, thank you,* and asking to have someone pass an item rather than reaching across the table. Because we have adults at the table, it is also important to remind them not to take so much of something that others don't get any.

This latter issue has been managed vigilantly. Some of our sons have lived in other countries where rice or potatoes are a staple of every meal. As a result, they love rice and potatoes of any kind and tend to heap their plates. We have learned to plan ahead to accommodate larger portions of these items. It also helps to remind them they are not the only ones at the table before covering their plates with three cups of rice.

One never knows when having good manners will make a difference in later life. A number of years ago, Clark accompanied one of our sons on an athletic recruiting trip to a respected university. During the visit, which included a number of other potential recruits and their parents, we were guests at a catered dinner on campus. During the dinner, Clark noticed several of the young recruits exhibiting extremely poor manners and etiquette. He discussed this with our son. Afterwards Clark had the opportunity to visit with the head football coach. During the conversation, he asked the coach what he looks for in players during on-campus recruiting visits. The coach's answer caught Clark by surprise. The coach said he watches the recruit's table manners during dinner. He further stated that he had found in his long coaching career that a recruit with good manners is more likely to exhibit discipline, respect team rules, and stay out of trouble. That, he said, is a better indicator than athleticism of whether a recruit will succeed. What a great lesson for a young man!

During dinner we talk about anything and everything, although we try to keep away from negative subjects. This would include poor grades, missing school assignments, or poor test results for example. Family dinners are not a time for lectures or chastisement. It is also not a time when punishments should be administered. There are other times to address these matters in a more respectful, productive, and usually private setting.

However, most topics are open season, and we laugh a lot. We especially like to ask questions that illicit inner feelings. This isn't always successful, but we are often surprised to get more than the typical one-word answers. We are usually intrigued by where the conversations go.

There is one other thing we do that helps set the tone and puts everyone in a proper frame of mind. Someone is called upon to pray. It is not a rote memorized statement but a heartfelt expression of gratitude for blessings and protection and especially for those who have sacrificed that we might have dinner together. Anyone at the table may be called upon to pray. It is pretty hard to have bad feelings when the family begins together in this manner.

One of the unintended positive results of regular family dinners has been the interest our children have in making dinner or dessert themselves. Some years ago, Leah's oldest bio-son started telling her about some of the dinners he had been making for his wife as well as dinners they had made together. He explained how much he loved taking a recipe and changing some of the ingredients to make it his own.

Leah was pleasantly surprised to hear he so enjoyed making meals and asked him where this newfound hobby came from. He said, "Well, Mom, you were always in the kitchen making food when I was growing up, so I guess it got me interested." Even though Leah didn't have her kids in the kitchen helping her make meals or desserts on a regular basis, it obviously had a positive impact. Leah's other bio-sons have also enjoyed making specific meals and desserts. Dinner can be a creative, artistic experience. But it can also become satisfying service to others. It helps foster both unconditional love and meaningful binding relationships that are critical in blended families.

On the Path Together

Several of our family members enjoy mountain biking, and the Rockies provide nearly endless opportunities to test our skill.

One mountain biking principle learned the hard way applies to our blended family experience. The single-track trails we often ride together are strewn with embedded protruding rocks, roots, bumps, and dips. The best way to take on these obstacles is to raise your body slightly off the seat and power pedal over them. This preserves the tailbone from uncomfortable bruises and allows the biker to smooth his or her ride while using less energy in the process. These lessons can be taught by an experienced rider to a novice, or the novice can learn the painful truth on their own. It is better to have an experienced guide. This principle is not different in raising children in a blended family. The parents must be available to provide that guidance when needed.

We recently took a trip to Moab, Utah in the heart of red rock country. Its world-famous, slick-rock bike trails provide stunning, other-worldly views. The area offers literally dozens of single-track mountain biking options. They roll along everything from the edge of two-thousand-foot cliffs to picturesque valleys studded with red rock formations and arches. The trails have been marked similar to those at ski resorts. A green circle for less difficult, a blue square for more difficult, and a black diamond for most difficult provide critical information.

We carefully reviewed the trails before our trip. Trails were chosen that fit the skill and experience of our group to ensure we did not get into terrain that was over anyone's head. This ensured an enjoyable time for all. There is a subtle danger for the careless or unprepared traveler who does not research the trails. Most of the trails look tame at the beginning but may have challenging or dangerous terrain along the way.

The poorly prepared group can find itself faced with long walks, accidents, serious injury, dehydration, or worse. It goes without saying that it is best to know as much as possible about the trail you plan to travel. The key to remember is that a rider cannot judge a trail's difficulty by simply looking at the first hundred yards. Our communication and quantity time principles provide important guideposts that will help the reader identify the most difficult blended-family terrain. Haphazard efforts will rarely produce a positive result in either a biking trip or raising healthy children.

Time together is critical to healthy family blending. Most quality time happens as quantity time occurs. There are numerous opportunities for families to establish patterns that allow quality experiences during hectic schedules. However, it must be a high priority and requires conscious effort from every member. Parents must make a commitment to develop consistent patterns of family time. Dinners, bedtime patterns, weekly family evenings and activities, observance of religious customs or secular traditions, and attending each other's activities all have a positive impact. Parents must lead this effort by example and adjust their schedules to be involved.

The initial transition to providing quantity time that allows quality time can be difficult. But once the patterns are set, they become part of family life; children grow to expect and even plan for it. We enjoy those moments when our children follow up on us to make sure we have not forgotten one of our usual activities. You know you are making progress when they take ownership and it becomes the children's pattern too.

Chapter VIII

Principle #7: The Pedestal

Why Marriage Anyway?

Within our combined sixty-eight years of blended family life, we have developed some experience dealing with difficult relationships. It has produced a kind of sixth sense that helps us recognize such challenges in other marriages. It has allowed us to deal more calmly with sudden change and provided an effective early-warning mechanism in our relationship. We have not hung out a sign to provide marriage advice, nor do we actively solicit such opportunities. However, we have been approached on occasion by struggling individuals or couples. Lack of attention to this principle is one of the most common issues we have found.

Marriage is still, according to a 2010 Pew Research Center survey, primarily entered into for love (93%), seeking lifelong commitment (87%), companionship (81%), children (59%), and financial stability (31%). The responses of those cohabitating are statistically close to those of married couples. The key societal change to the institution is in the nature and viability of the underlying commitment to unconditionally deliver on the above.

Increases in serial cohabitating partners, non-traditional families, and divorce are testing the boundaries and role of marriage in society. A growing casualness toward commitment and over-emphasis on physical gratification constitute major threats. Studies cited in chapter one confirm that couples are increasingly entering into less-permanent, convenience-oriented relationships. It is possible that some of the same needs described in the survey above are temporarily satisfied. However, these looser, careless commitments do not bode well in achieving long-term stability for the affected adults or children.

Modern couples are more frequently choosing to forego the commitment aspect of marriage completely. This cannot help but encourage self-orientation in the relationship. It is no surprise that relationships where the couple has given themselves permission not to be fully committed often fail. Regardless of the couple's intentions, they are less likely to experience long-term success if they choose to hold onto a *me*-oriented focus. Such arrangements can be managed when everything is going well. But what happens to it under stress?

Extended family, financial, job loss, infidelity and relationship conflict, hanging out with single friends, illness, accidents, addictions, and child-discipline issues produce such tests. What incentive does a couple have to deal with inconvenience or conflict when it boils down to emptying out a closet and a few drawers?

Blended families need a long-term, selfless, committed attitude. An arrangement based on a casual foundation too easily transitions from roommate pleasantries to bad roommates and finally to going separate ways. If children are involved, it tends to strain a questionable commitment thus multiplying its complexities. The resulting damage can be generational.

Why is commitment important? Can non-traditional situations be just as committed as traditional marriage? Of course, this is possible. In addition, the previously shared statistics indicate that many marriages and remarriages can also end badly. Even if the relationship begins well, the challenge of convincing children, who have already been badly burned by relationship breakups, that this time it will be stable is perhaps the major obstacle. Successful family blending depends primarily on a stable and steadfast relationship between the custodial parents. Stability is dramatically improved by the strength of the couple's commitment. That should be viewed as foundational to mastery of the principles presented in this book.

If a couple is not willing to make a serious, permanent commitment and stand behind it, what are they saying to each other? What promises are they making to the children? Blending a family is not a time for shortcuts, test periods, one-week stands, or cutting corners on devotion or commitment. With children it sometimes doesn't even matter what it really is, blended parents can lose them with the developing situations' initial appearance. Sometimes the important question is, "What does it look and feel like?" rather than "What is it?" That is why the dating process has more intense demands. Don't go against the odds, especially when children are involved. There is too much at stake.

The Better Way

Robert Frost was one of the most critically acclaimed American poets of the twentieth century. His best-known poem, *The Road Not Taken,* ends with these five lines.

> *I shall be telling this with a sigh*
> *Somewhere ages and ages hence:*
> *Two roads diverged in a wood, and I—*
> *I took the one less traveled by,*
> *And that has made all the difference.*

It is important to establish a different, more reliable precedent from the beginning in any blended-family endeavor. It is not the easier road, but it will make all the difference. It absolutely must feel permanent to the couple and each one of the children. Many of the principles already discussed will help. But there is one overriding focus that must be present for long-term success to be ensured. The couple must love each other unconditionally and consistently. This means you cannot enter into a relationship haphazardly with careless commitments and muddied, selfish goals. We have said a blended family marriage must be all-in. But it goes farther than that. Placing each other on a pedestal of respect, admiration, and appreciation is the essence of achieving the level of commitment necessary to endure difficult times.

This means you cannot hesitate to speak openly with children about strong mutual feelings. Do not be shy if your children see a little public display of affection once in a while. One of these moments occurred shortly after our marriage. It has become a family legend. One of our sons caught us hugging and sneaking a kiss in the kitchen. He turned to leave, a bit embarrassed. One of us said quickly before he walked out, "We're just having a little argument." It was not long afterward that another of our children caught us embracing and called out, "Mom and Dad are arguing again."

The phrase became part of our family lexicon. Our kids know that hugging is not our way of arguing, of course. It is a fun way of downplaying our children's reaction to parental displays of affection. We consider it a compliment and will often ask our children to excuse us while we argue for a moment.

It seems like a silly example but consider what happened as a result. It is the little things— the brief moments—that children remember forever. Our children have reinforced in their minds that we love each other and that harsh language, raised voices, and heated arguments are not part of our home. This does not mean we avoid all disagreements or differences of opinion. We certainly have some. But we talk them out in a calm and reasoned manner. In addition, we refrain from keeping score or dredging up old wounds and grievances. When there is a problem to be solved or a discouraging event to deal with, we are there for each other. Because we don't allow communication during these tense moments to become distracted by history or gratuitous emotion, we can focus on the problem at hand and solve it together.

Perhaps the most difficult moment in our marriage was navigated without an argument at all. However, it was not without pain, embarrassment, and significant penitence. A couple of years after we had finished the basement, including a bedroom, our moment of personal challenge occurred. Clark noticed a dry patch of grass where the sprinklers did not reach near one of the basement window wells. He put a rotating sprinkler head on the end of our hose and turned it on to water the area. Unfortunately, he forgot about it, and two days later Leah went down to the basement bedroom to look for something. It was being used for storage at the time.

Her feet squished on the rug as she entered the room. A ripple rolled over an inch-deep layer of water that covered the entire room and was threatening to spread to other rooms. She called Clark down, and they immediately observed that the window well had over a foot of standing water in it. The window looked like an aquarium from the inside. The water was running through spaces in the window down the newly painted wall to the floor. Clark realized his error and turned the hose off. He retrieved a small water pump from the shed and tossed it into the well to empty the standing water.

Leah was in tears and didn't say much in the moment. She explained later that she decided it was better not to say anything because it "wouldn't have been very nice." Besides, she knew Clark felt terrible also. We all have times when we need to follow the timeworn rule, if you can't say something nice, don't say anything at all. This rule plays an important role in all healthy relationships. We immediately set to work getting everything out of the wet bedroom, including some paper items which couldn't be saved. When catastrophe strikes, taking one step at a time together usually gets us both through to the other side without unnecessary collateral relationship damage.

Thus began a several-days reclamation project, assisted by two of our sons, first to empty and dry out the contents. We then removed and discarded the ruined carpet and padding. Finally, we mopped, shop-vacuumed, and dried out the affected rooms. Words are insufficient to describe the horrible mess. Leah is a trooper in difficult situations, but this was too traumatic. After getting the contents removed from the room, she was unable to look at it and rarely reentered the basement until the work was nearly done. She focused her efforts on the frustrating process of finding new carpet that matched the remainder of the unaffected rooms and a contractor to replace drywall and repaint.

We discovered later that the sprinkler was not directly spraying the window well. However, it was close enough, in combination with a natural conduit in the clay-like soil and the length of time, to do the terrible job. The interesting part, which illustrates our family atmosphere, was that there were no recriminations, accusations, or arguments. Emotions ran close to the surface for several days. However, fault was clear and accepted. The problem was addressed without distracting emotional strife. There were, of course, conversations and learning involved. But these occurred through calm discussion of the situation and not via in-the-moment, emotion-laden civil war. The hose has never again been placed that close to the window well. Better for the grass to suffer.

A traumatic event is easier to face when a couple has created a solid foundation of daily acts—recognition, appreciation, and love. When the bigger challenges must be faced, it is done together from a stable base. This allows a couple to overcome even the darkest moments. It is a little like the way a well-conditioned athlete recovers from a serious injury.

The athlete's body is strong. The muscles, tendons, and joints work in concert with healthy organs and internal systems. This may serve to limit the severity of an injury while promoting more rapid recovery. The healthy mental makeup, attitude, and lifestyle of the respective athlete can also contribute to rapid recovery. This translates into a higher level of discipline, which contributes to a faster and more complete rehab. It is not only about who the person is physically, it is also about who they have become mentally, emotionally, and spiritually.

The same is true of a healthy, loving, committed marriage. The couple engages in a daily exercise of the principles of love, kindness, admiration, gratitude, respect, and acknowledgment. This goes a long way to ensuring they are on the same page when difficulties arise. In turn, it allows them to be better prepared to deal with traumatic events, not just enduring the event but recovering and learning from it.

Small Things Matter Most

We both go out of our way to remember anniversaries, birthdays, and other milestones. However, Clark also surprises Leah regarding the smaller, less-remembered anniversaries in their relationship. These include their first date, their initial secret engagement, their formal engagement, their first meeting, and other more obscure but significant moments. These are easy to overlook by couples as the years together lengthen. Leah also keeps the relationship fun with unpredictable acts of love.

We enjoy being together, perhaps to a fault. During a recent summer Leah was responsible for taking a group of about twenty-five twelve- to eighteen-year-old girls to summer camp. She was gone for a few days. Being apart like this leaves an empty space in both our hearts regardless of how much we may enjoy the particular activity. Upon her return, after the camping equipment was dried out and put away, we enjoyed about an hour of quiet sharing. We talked of her experiences, challenges, success, and satisfying accomplishments. Listening to each other's deepest feelings creates tender bonding moments.

So far we have emphasized that through consistent emphasis on small daily caring acts, a couple can set a pattern by which they can bind their lives together. However, big events are important too. We also enjoy engaging in surprises for each other for mainstream events.

One example made a lifelong impact on a teenage son who at the time was struggling more than we realized. It was 2006 and the date of our first anniversary. Among the fun exchange of notes and activities surrounding our anniversary, Clark surprised Leah with thirteen roses. The arrangement consisted of twelve beautiful deep-red long-stem roses and one long stem white rose.

Leah guessed the message immediately, but our son asked why one rose was different. Clark told him that each red rose was for a month of our marriage and the white rose was for the eternity we look forward to sharing together. Tears immediately filled his eyes. This young man had endured two divorces, multiple moves, and repeatedly having to reconstruct his life.

We had not considered the impact on a fourteen-year-old when it dawned on him that he could live his life going forward like a normal kid. The implication of our commitment for him was far more powerful than we anticipated. It meant for perhaps the first time in his life, he could look forward to a stable home environment where he could thrive and grow. It was a powerful moment.

Seven years later when he returned from living twenty-four months in Honduras, the impact was still with him. Upon his return, he presented us with an approximately two-foot-square wood carving especially made for us by a Honduran artisan. In a semi-circle across the top were carved thirteen roses with twelve of them colored red and the center one painted white. They hung like clouds over a panel carving of the building where our marriage was solemnized. The carving included our names and the date of our eternal commitment. It was a moving and tender reminder of the impact we unknowingly had made on him years before. This beautiful work of art is displayed prominently where we are reminded each day of our great blessings.

The Bio-Parental Relationship

As part of building a sure foundation upon which a blended family can thrive, parents must be sensitive to differing dynamics. Subtle signals can warn of formidable obstacles. One of the potentially most significant is what we will refer to as the bio-parental relationship. It is the obverse side of the bio-compass discussed earlier.

As parents you strive to love each of your children completely and without preference. It means treating children individually and fairly. That is very different than treating them the same. Their lives and needs are not one-size-fits-all. Each interaction must be customized to those needs. Parents can be successful by recognizing that it plays out daily and forever.

However, it is also important to realize that any parent will harbor deep, long-developed feelings for their bio-children. Such experiential-based bonding is a fact of living life together and raising them from infancy. Bio-parents become bonded through birth and child-rearing in ways that may never be able to be duplicated with stepchildren. Such bonding pre-dates the blended family. There is nothing wrong with this. Please understand we believe strongly that one can love bio- and stepchildren with equal intensity. However, the fact that these bio-parental feelings exist creates a volatile mix. This mix can be vigorously stirred when introduced into the family blender. It can be stirred again if the family brings additional children into the picture through natural birth or adoption.

The blended couple must respect the existence of these deep bio-parental feelings. They are produced by a natural process of experiencing life's roller coaster. They are not negative to the individual experiencing them nor are they necessarily negative to the family. However, they can be hard to express, explain, or even recognize until brought to the surface by events. Such deep, protective feelings may catch the bio-parent as well as their spouse by surprise.

If addressed in an unhealthy or divisive way, these feelings can set the stage for family strife. They must be acknowledged and sensitively managed, or they will plant seeds that could eventually grow into damaging division. Yet, if identified, discussed, and embraced, they will become an asset to the blending process. Examples of times when the depth of the bio-parental relationship can be revealed include discipline, rules, dating, children's friend choices, religious participation, financial assistance, grandchildren, interaction with former spouses, trust and expanding privileges, setting standards of behavior, second chances, and compromises.

Acknowledgement in open communication is key to dealing with this issue. The spouse or other children may construe the bio-parent's interaction as favoritism. This must be anticipated and diffused by honest open communication. Take some private time with your spouse or the child. Confirm your unconditional love and commitment to each while frankly acknowledging the instinctive bio-parent feelings that you are working to manage. Ask for their thoughts. You can work on it together. It will turn a dangerous potential wedge into an opportunity to bond.

Implementation strategies are similar to the bio-compass principle in chapter five. These are times when first-level, direct interaction with the bio-child in question should come from the bio-parent with the support of the stepparent. It takes a tremendous amount of humility to be a backup parent in this situation. The ability not to insert yourself unless necessary is a gift to your spouse and children. While patiently standing by, you should actively listen and be prepared if asked for input. The bio-parent also needs to be sensitive and include their spouse to help ease the transition. This will strengthen overall blended relationships.

There is one final element to navigating these tricky waters. If you or your spouse have these deeper bio-parental feelings, they must be respected. The bio-parent may be more protective of the bio-child's actions or statements. Discipline may be limited to the bio-parent at the beginning. These conditions cannot be forced. Understand that family blending also requires tough transitioning for parents.

The stepparent can expand his/her role as time goes on and trust builds. Patience and a humble approach are key. If the person you are dating has a temper, is insecure, or easily offended, consider these as red flags that will slow or prevent critical blending transitions.

Parents must still be vigilant not to create an unintended caste system that drives wedges between their bio-, half- and stepchildren. Your children must work at crossing the bridge and seeing each other as siblings. They must do it in their time and way. Parents can, by their example, ease that passage.

However, it is possible, especially if the children are older, that they will never perfectly blend. They have their own lives after all. Maybe they will never be best buddies. But parents can work to create a comfortable, respectful, and safe environment where everyone can enjoy each other. Each child may still experience a differing mix of feelings, which must be recognized and incorporated. Yet your actions and general example must always speak to the foundation that exists. Your blended family will be healthier if your children know they are valued, loved, and judged on their own merits rather than their biological origin.

Committed blended parents will create an environment of unconditional love that everyone will feel. Their commitment will openly acknowledge that natural paternal or maternal feelings exist. They will work to manage them successfully. The extra measure of respect and patience parents extend to each other will have a daily impact on how they interact with their children. Approaching potentially volatile events on a basis of previous discussion and planning will enhance relationships, avoid traps, reduce surprises, and eliminate hurtful interactions. These constitute the wiser road taken. Its blessings will impact the family for *ages hence.*

CHAPTER IX

Principle #8: The Family Cornerstone

Blended Awareness

We have already mentioned that our family enjoys cycling. Our community affords many miles of paved and unpaved trails. Paved bike trails tend to be fairly clear of obstructions, but a portion of every road ride includes regular streets. A bike rider notices things to which auto drivers on the same route are completely oblivious. Gravel, debris, cracks, and small potholes that can cause major problems for a cyclist will go mostly unnoticed by those in larger vehicles. A pothole might cause a driver to cringe and curse. A cyclist hitting the same pothole could pop a tire or cause a crash, sustaining a serious personal injury or extensive damage.

A cyclist also must have heightened awareness regarding traffic, side roads, driveways, signage, intersections, and others using the roadway. This is not to say that those in cars are not careful; it's just that there is a higher degree of care necessary for a cyclist when sharing the road with larger, heavier vehicles. It is literally a matter of life and death.

Blended families must also be more vigilant regarding their path, obstacles, and threats than more traditional family situations. We are not suggesting that such vigilance is not beneficial for traditional families. The principles apply to everyone, but parents in a blended family must notice small things that others miss. A blended family is not business as usual. Everything is magnified, increasing its intensity. Children in a blended family may have emotions or insecurities that linger closer to the surface. Their self-esteem and sense of worth may be more fragile. In addition, loyalties may be confused or self-confidence eroded. They usually have a well-developed sense of skepticism regarding parental promises or commitments that don't pass the smell test. This places greater emphasis on recognizing difficulties early and, when wounds occur, being available during the healing process.

Much has been said in previous chapters regarding the importance of a solid, dependable foundation. Every foundation begins with the laying of a cornerstone. It is the cornerstone that determines the orientation and leads to the layout of the base footings of any structure.

A flaw in the cornerstone or footings can eventually lead to weakness in the entire structure. Further, if a contractor is careless in pouring or reinforcing the basement concrete, the result may not bear the intended weight properly. There are occasional examples of auto or pedestrian bridges, observation decks, or suspended seating that have collapsed due to excessive weight, flawed design, or careless construction. In addition, there is a program of earthquake reinforcement by states and the federal government focused on hospitals, schools, bridges, and other public buildings. It is a response to the perception of greater earthquake risk exposure for inadequate or unreinforced structures.

Clark built a home in the foothills north of Salt Lake City, Utah over twenty-five years ago. It was a three-story Georgian brick home that recalls early American Colonial architecture. The concrete was poured during a period of severe winter storms in the early 1990s. Within a single month, the area suffered two massive storms, each dropping in excess of forty-eight inches of snow within a twenty-four-hour period on the hillside bench. He remembers the contractor using a snowblower to clear off the foundation, so the basement walls could be formed and poured.

While watching the walls being poured, he noticed the northeast corner included large chunks of ice mixed in with the warm concrete pour. He inquired but was told it would melt and cause no problems.

After about a year he noticed that during the spring melt and after prolonged rainfall, the basement carpet would become wet. Further examination, with the help of the contractor, revealed a hole clean through the foundation about six feet above its base in the northeast corner of the basement wall. This hole allowed water to flow freely into the home during periods when the clay soil's ability to absorb the runoff was overcome by the amount of water building up around the foundation. As the saturation level rose to the height of the hole, water flowed through the foundation wall into the basement room. The flaw was patched and tarred successfully, eliminating the problem.

The contractor determined that the flaw was created by a chunk of ice on the day it was poured. The ice melted after the concrete set, leaving a hole. Foundational flaws may not be immediately apparent. Whether the flaw will produce nagging inconvenience, significant problems, or result in a catastrophic collapse depends on its nature, location, and degree of stress.

However, over time with added stress, severe events or normal wear and tear, the structure is likely to reveal the flaw. The concept does not differ within the family unit.

What Page Are You On?

Families can be supported by a strong, stable base from the start or reinforced later as necessary. Either way, the strength of the foundation is dependent on a cornerstone of adherence to basic principles of establishing and nourishing family values. These must be dependable, steadfast, and based reliably on truth. A solid structure of dependable family values, combined with involvement in a community that reinforces and nourishes them, are key ingredients of an enduring foundation.

Too often we see these critical family underpinnings discarded or carelessly maintained. This promotes personal and family vulnerability. A haphazard or inconsistent family value system often has these voids filled by counterfeit materials constructed from convenient, ever-changing, pop-culture mythology.

A couple should discuss their beliefs, background, goals, attitudes, and values as part of the courting process. We have often heard others comment, "If only someone had told me that before I got married." The fact is that someone probably did, but when emotions cloud the picture, listening often goes out the window. An ounce of avoidance is truly worth years of trying to deal with family strife. Even a limited effort to examine shared belief systems can allow a relationship to avoid playing an endless game of blended family Whack-A-Mole.

Emotion is a powerful and necessary part of any relationship. But it can also create emotional fog, making it difficult to be objective. This is especially true if the relationship becomes physical too quickly. We have taught our children that there is an important and sacred role for the intimate side of a marriage relationship. Physical intimacy can be a powerful aspect of marital bonding at any age. However, this same power can also overwhelm natural relationship development doing serious long-term damage if it dominates courtship interactions.

Physical involvement can easily engender a self-focus, which overwhelms, stunts, or prevents relationship growth by replacing it with a transient counterfeit. The critical foundation a couple depends on can be left underdeveloped, displaced, or deformed. It is too often the reason a rebound or live-in relationship runs into later dysfunction. Some will dismiss this advice as unenlightened or Victorian. But based on our observations and experience, they do this at their own peril.

Intimate relations are a sensitive and intensely personal topic. Some may disagree with our position. It is always possible you are the exception. However, playing against the odds in blended families usually proves unwise in the long-term. And family blending is all about the long-term.

It seems obvious when you see a couple who are not on the same page regarding this and other key principles. "The train wreck is only a matter of time, why can't they see it?" we ask ourselves. Somehow the thrill of the ride dampens common sense and inspirational insight until after the fact.

We were pulled aside at a community dinner one evening by a couple who were seriously considering a blended-family marriage. The situation had been complicated by premature intimacy although we did not know that at the time. It only took a few minutes for us to identify a number of child-rearing and relationship issues over which they had strongly differing points of view. Our advice was that they work to find common ground, so their relationship could flourish. They were never able to address their differences and the relationship ended bitterly.

As tough as the experience must have been for them, it was far better than getting married and then divorcing. A dating couple will benefit in the long-term by including a healthy dose of experience, open conversation, and understanding as they get to know each other better.

Being on the same page has a powerful impact on a couple's ability to achieve a sound, dependable marriage. Open communication is important in promoting this process. But discussion alone is not enough. The couple can learn much about each other from the way they approach living their individual lives. Sufficient shared experience should also occur enabling each to determine whether the professed values stand up in practice prior to bringing two families together.

Foundational Value Systems

We will return briefly to the GPS analogy used in an earlier chapter. The technology provides a standard that, if in-sync, gives helpful directional information. Our oldest son is a pilot and flight instructor as previously stated. He explained one evening that the GPS system must be regularly maintained and fine-tuned. A department in the United States Air Force is responsible for making these adjustments. The accuracy of the satellites that provide GPS coordinates depends on regular adjustments to timing mechanisms that are uploaded. If this is not done every couple of weeks, the GPS system is rendered inaccurate and undependable. Like GPS, the dependability of a family's shared belief system erodes quickly if not continuously maintained and fine-tuned.

Having common religious beliefs or attending the same church are often pointed to as solid indicators of long-term stability. Such shared experience offers a family the opportunity for regular adjustments to remain finely tuned. If these beliefs are strongly and jointly held, they can be a powerful unifier. However, sharing religious beliefs does not guarantee that the couple is on the same page when it comes to their practice.

Successful family blending goes far beyond religious membership or upbringing. It is intertwined with how you and your prospective spouse live your lives. Is your practical application of beliefs moving you in a similar direction? Are you both working on the same goals? Is what you are becoming during this life's journey compatible? This is true in the secular world as well. If religious practice is not part of your family's culture, then this void must be filled by something that binds you together in a credible and endurable fashion. However, even when a couple shares similar secular values, it is wise to subject them to the same pre-nuptial examination. Simply having similar professed world or political views is different than how they are applied in practice.

So what are we referring to? The answer is that any successful family must have a set of consistently lived foundational values and beliefs. These create the framework for pulling together when dealing with life. They must be formalized in some way. It is good if parents base them on vows, promises, and mutual commitment. However, the best results are centered in a recognized covenanting partnership between the couple and the divine. These should be reinforced by a regular support framework within and surrounding the family.

In our case it was actively nourished by regular daily, weekly, and monthly behaviors. We decided that there were several things we had to do faithfully to interweave our blending with a solid foundational belief system. These included regular family and individual prayer and Scripture study; consistent participation in proscribed church meetings, activities, and service; weekly family time; and daily dinners. These may seem like small things, but they have led our family to much greater heights of unity and satisfaction. We also believe it has helped our children see our home as a safe harbor from the world.

Families do not face severe trials every day. As a result, we may be tempted to put off creating this framework. After all it takes time and much effort. However, major issues may be developing just below the surface as we are lulled into complacency. Our current pleasant view can lead us to believe that the sky will always be free from threatening storms.

But complacency can prevent a couple from building a sure foundation. Believing what we have is good enough for now may not be good at all. When the severe tests arrive on the doorstep, it is too late. Families cannot flip a switch, suddenly becoming something they are not. If you have made this mistake, all is not lost. You may have to endure a terrible storm. But it is never too late to take your lumps, make better choices, and chart a new and more stable course.

Blended families in particular have members that are struggling to recreate structure in their lives. Whether these catastrophic changes have happened gradually or in one sudden earthshaking event, there is a tendency to become skeptical that anything will ever be stable again. Therefore, half-measures or convenient self-serving constructs cannot withstand close scrutiny. These sensitivities raise the bar in the minds of blended family members, making it tougher to accept casual or inconsistent values.

Parents stack the deck against success when the necessary framework is absent. Children see through constantly changing backdrops in which standards depend on power, convenience, negotiating skill, mood, who can yell the loudest or make the biggest threats, physical strength, misplaced priorities, selfishness, lazy inattention, avoidance of engagement, contention, how stressful the day has been, willingness to accept or sidestep responsibility, or whether one really cares. You can expect that children entering into a blended family probably already have extensive knowledge in identifying what does not work.

A blended family that already shares a traditional, spiritual, or religious belief system will discover this is a good start to building an essential framework. However, such beliefs must be a regular part of life. A one-hour-per-week or twice-a-year belief system will not provide the foundation needed. Neither will a random or arbitrary code of nebulous spiritualism. Children are more successful if their fences are dependable, even if they occasionally disagree and would like to shift the fence line.

This approach runs contrary to a popular societal trend which aims to dismiss organized religion as a corrupt, control-oriented bureaucracy. This destructive counterfeit degrades both home and community-based beliefs as if anything organized is somehow inherently wrong. This pop-culture trend creates a void it attempts to fill with ill-defined concepts of personal goodness or spirituality. Religious organizations exist because none of us can make it alone. We, in fact, need each other and are benefitted and supported by the experience. A family that surrounds itself with a community of external support and caring individuals reinforces their own foundations.

We realize what we are suggesting may not be generally popular or politically correct to some in today's world. Our culture is infused with attitudes of skepticism that make a dependable family belief system appear constrictive or controlling. It is in fact the opposite in our experience. Strongly held and shared beliefs and values produce personal freedom to pursue uplifting goals while releasing family members from many of the emotional, spiritual, and physical burdens that otherwise may hold them back. In fact, a foundational value system will never work if it is an excuse to control or dominate. It must be something that is arrived at individually as well as collectively. It is most influential when accompanied by each member's personal conviction that such family values originate from a higher source.

The Basics

If you do not share spiritual or religious beliefs, you can still work to create manageable foundations. Your family may choose to base these on common values as long as they remain consistent. These alternative foundations are more difficult to support but may be reasonably based on family or cultural traditions, patriotism, a shared family business, or a set of basic virtues. The challenge with these alternative systems is they tend to change with time and family circumstances. Having your family's foundation rooted in a solid conviction is more permanent and reliable.

The key to permanence is that your shared family values must include six basic components:

1. They are adhered to and reinforced by daily example and practice.

2. They help children and adults answer the *Why?* questions, not just the *What?*

3. They have substance and practical application. In other words, they work even when they differ from or are challenged by practices of others, sometimes the majority of others.

4. They are dependable and not subject to random change. This means they generally originate from some higher source.

5. Each member must do their part to personally nourish the foundation of their values through study, prayer, and application. A belief system is never static and must be actively nourished or it will fade.

6. They must be uplifting and stabilizing.

For example, if parents teach their children that being honest with themselves and others is of critical importance, they must do their best to live it every day. It does not mean you do it perfectly, but you must sincerely try. Parents and children must be forthright with each other, teachers, employers, friends, the government, etc. They cannot deceive or mislead. In addition, it cannot exist in a vacuum and must be lived in combination with other principles of equal weight to the family.

Honesty without tact, kindness, or consideration toward others is not a virtue. We have occasionally met some who flaunt their frankness. They wear it as a badge of honor and seem to glory in being rude. They might justify it because they "speak their mind," or "tell it like it is." They may give themselves permission by stating, "That's just the way I am," or "I'm willing to say things others are not." It is important to recognize that being honest does not mean eliminating all civilized filters. We do not give voice to every thought that pops into our heads. Being rude isn't being honest or frank, it's just being rude. This is simply lazy communication laced with hubris.

The Critical *Why*

Being able to answer the *why* question is an important part of any sure foundation. Society is full of *what* happens, *what* people think, *what* one should or should not do, or *what* label a person has. It is the easiest way to communicate. "Don't do that because I said so!" That is a double *what*: "Do *what* I want because of *what* I said." It is neither quality communication nor an example of sound foundational values.

What communication is easy but tends to be the most superficial type of interaction. It is the basis of political fearmongering, misleading rumors, and innuendo. We hear what happened on the news. We read about it on the internet. When we are fed only the *what,* we are left to speculate on the rest of the story. If we are not careful, we teach only that behavior to our children. When we teach the *what* of a subject, we normally tell them what will happen if they do or don't do something. Parents have a responsibility to teach beyond the *what*.

For example, we may remind our teen that arriving home after the agreed-upon curfew will result in a consequence. In our family that consequence is understood and agreed upon. It means they are to be home early on the next comparable night. There is nothing wrong with such *what* instruction, especially when delivered kindly and agreed to. However, this superficial level of communication falls short in helping them understand how to plan for and avoid the situation. An additional *why* element is needed.

What is the least important part of the reason for a curfew. Parents must discuss with the teen *why* this rule is important and *why* it applies to his or her life. In our family we have rules of conduct that help develop trust and responsibility. Curfews are part of this. Adhering to an agreed-upon curfew builds self-discipline, confidence, and responsibility. It demonstrates an inward commitment and builds trust. Expansion of privileges is not based on age, rather privileges are dependent on the measure of trust we have in each specific child.

In addition, the risks associated with incidents of crime, accidents, or getting into unintended or questionable moral situations statistically increase as the evening grows later. The risk of unintended difficulties increases as young people get tired, let their guard down, and the scheduled date activities end and teens improvise. The teen is their own best teacher. They do this by practicing discipline in using common sense, following directions, and obeying rules. As they do, they grow in maturity and self-reliance and build a reservoir of trust and confidence with their parents. This in turn leads to additional privileges or being given the benefit of the doubt if something does happen to disrupt their timing one evening.

This principle also plays out in school. Our children know if their teachers believe they care about the coursework, then when the time comes that they need to be given the benefit of the doubt, they are more likely to get it. These are compelling *why* explanations to the *what* rule.

Why Opens the Door to *How*

It is important to understand that *why* also opens the door to a young person's ability to problem solve. When family members understand the *why,* they can more effectively go about *how* they can develop the behavior necessary for personal success. In the school setting example, it is important for the students to do the little things they are asked to build a teacher's belief that they care. If they arrive on time, are attentive, interested, ask questions, finish homework, and give testing their best effort, an atmosphere is created that says they care. Any good teacher will recognize this. Then when something is missed or a mistake is made and they initiate follow-up with the teacher, it will be better received. The payoff comes when they discover the teacher gives them the benefit of the doubt. This is called trust.

Developing these traits and habits as children will extend to displaying the same behaviors as adults. A person who develops a caring attitude is blessed in countless other ways as they grow. Having an attitude of caring translates to developing healthy relationships at work, with family, and with friends. It is also an important part of helping children in blended families rebuild confidence. These are all important *whys*.

It is true that not all teachers get it. But our children have always been better off when they sincerely cared. Parents can be important in helping children demonstrate responsible behavior by helping them understand ahead of time *why* they should care. This leads naturally to the next step—*how* to go about it. Sometimes parents are too quick in excusing the *what* behavior and thus enable their children in sidestepping responsibility and opportunities for growth. It is easy to fall into the habit of writing the tardy excuse every day for *what* they are doing rather than building better behavior by teaching them *why* it is important to be on time and *how* to do it.

Our daughter kept sleeping through her alarm. It did not help that it played soft ocean sounds and bird calls when it went off. It also was a digital nightmare to set correctly. Clark bought her an old-style face clock with an alarm, consisting of a small hammer that banged on two bells above the clock. It was loud and obnoxious, and she only had to pull out a single button to set it. We were worried that such a gift might be a little offensive. She jumped with joy upon opening the box. We were confused. It definitely was not that cool. However, she had never seen a mechanical alarm clock before. She told us it was the coolest new retro-technology ever. Go figure!

What Do You Dwell On?

We live in a society where individuals are often encouraged or incentivized to dwell on the *what*. Too many are obsessed with their own victimization, entitlement, or right to something that they have not worked to obtain. It does not matter if children are taught they are not responsible because of their race, religion, poverty, wealth, privilege, education, lack of education, genes, birth status, parental status, lifestyle choices, environment, or prospects. They learn how to dwell on their own victimization.

When society or parents do this, they reinforce the notion that children are helpless, hopeless victims that cannot do anything to change their situation. Children are left adrift, helplessly waiting for the next comet to hit and blame their problem on the comet. This is not to say that individuals can never become a victim. Certainly, bad stuff happens to everyone. However, society encourages us to feed attitudes of obsessively dwelling on gratuitous victimization. This includes manufacturing excuses that prevent us from taking responsibility. Taking responsibility empowers. Empowerment means we can change things. Oprah Winfrey stated it well when she said, "I know for sure that what we dwell on is who we become."

Positive and negative examples of obsessive, gratuitous victimization are all around us. Why is this a false narrative? Because we are always free to choose something different than we have if we are willing to work hard to achieve it. As we strive in this manner, we discover that success isn't just found in the endgame of achieving our goal. Rather, real success comes in the growth we experience as we climb. Something that is given to you can always be taken away. But something you have earned by the sweat of your brow—a degree, personal knowledge, or strengthened character and confidence—is yours forever.

We have tried to help our children practice empowering themselves by taking responsibility. This builds confidence. They know even when a mistake is made, they have the power to overcome it and do things differently the next time. We also reinforce that no matter what happens, we will never give up on them and they are always loved. Get them to dwell on positive, encouraging, and uplifting things, and that is who they will become.

Our children inevitably come to us at various times during the dating process with feelings of discouragement. They become fatigued with the demanding process of finding a compatible person who is actually interested in a relationship as well as having a fun time. It is easy to give up and drop out of the dating scene. Our responses have typically been to focus them on what they are learning about people and relationships during the process and why it will help them make better decisions further along their path.

We also remind them of what we call the first two Burbidge rules. First, members of our family have always had to work hard to achieve anything worthwhile. Second, when you've given up on the dating experience and are taking a break, that is most often when you stumble across that special someone. It is our goal to help them become empowered problem-solvers who never give up. This builds self-reliance, confidence, and a belief that they can tackle and accomplish hard things.

It Has to Work

Principles we teach to children must actually have practical application and work. In the cases cited, a person who is honest, willing to work hard, and demonstrates caring compassion is more often rewarded by others. Certainly, someone who acts like they do not care about their work or is found to be dishonest will not do well. The great trap of victimization and entitlement is that individuals are tempted to conclude that the fault lies with anyone or anything else but them. The resulting tragedy is that such beliefs not only keep them from overcoming, but they actually prevent them from learning. After all, there is nothing to learn if they had nothing whatsoever to do with the comet landing on them.

We have based our family value system on shared religious beliefs. These are beliefs that help effectively answer the *what, why,* and *how* questions so we may move forward together. Believing that a loving, approachable, and actively involved heavenly Father stands behind a revealed value system is a powerful enabler. It has allowed our children to personally test His reality and teachings. Through their own personal discovery our children have developed a firm and steadfast commitment.

We further believe that our presence here on Earth and in our blended family in particular is part of a plan. Our children know this plan allows for mistakes, correction, and repentance so that we may learn from experiential choices. Our lives have a purpose. They are not accidental. Most importantly, our blended family is an important vehicle by which we can pursue that purpose in a healthy and successful way.

This is not something that can or should be forced. It must come with each child's interest and search for meaning. But, because we believe God is real and have received numerous personal confirmations, we are confident our children can too. Examples of confidence and faith are powerful influencers, but personal experience imprints on a child's soul.

We have encouraged them to essentially exercise what we refer to as *The Spiritual Scientific Method*. They form and test the hypothesis and arrive at their own personal conviction regarding our family belief system, its divine source, and why that is important in their lives. We believe anyone with a sincere desire to know can do this. They must be open to any outcome and set aside their biases. A willingness to seek with a sincere desire to know can successfully test their beliefs.

During the early years of our marriage, one of our adult sons was struggling on strange paths. His struggles seem to have found their beginnings in the disruptive interactions with a previous stepparent. One of his many challenges included turning away from his connection to God. He remained communicative with us during this difficult period, although some of the conversations were frustrating. We had regular discussions with him covering a wide variety of subjects. It seemed that almost every week he was chasing after some new pop-culture craze. It was heartrending to watch him waste time and energy crashing into one dead end after another.

One recurring topic was his relationship with God. During one of these conversations, Clark challenged him. He said if he really had a sincere desire to know God, then it could happen. Our son finally seemed open to the concept and was ready to consider seeking a personal knowledge that God is real and cares about him. Clark explained that it was something personal between him and God and could happen quickly if the conditions were right. Our son was not ready at the time but was open to the conversation. Clark further challenged him to call when he was sincerely ready, and he would tell him how to do it. A few weeks later, Clark got a call. The conversation went something like this:

"Hi, do you have a minute?"

"Sure."

"Remember when you told me that anytime I wanted to know whether there is a God who cares about me I could call you and you'd tell me how to do it?"

"Yes."

"Well you don't have to tell me. I tested it for myself and I know."

It was a tender moment. Without having it explained, he had been guided to try *The Spiritual Scientific Method* for himself. It worked.

The results have been real, profound, and extraordinarily practical in our lives. It provides each family member with a critical framework that allows establishment of a cornerstone, footings, and firmly set foundation. Regular nourishment strengthens them to bear the burdens that will fall on their shoulders. Most important of all, our children feel empowered because they know we, and their Father in heaven, are always there to walk with them. They are never alone.

The Self-Worship Trap

An alarming current trend is what we will refer to as the *cult of self-worship*. It is much more subtle than narcissism and those engaged seldom see it for what it really is. We see it in the rejection, with only cursory inspection, of religious belief systems. This is often done without filling the resulting void. Because the human spirit yearns for something, individuals who have created this void often end up cobbling together their own convenient belief system.

The result can cover the entire spectrum from comforting impotency or innocent justification to destructive toxicity. These belief system constructs tend to justify already established behaviors and lifestyles. Self-worship tends by its nature to push the concept of God to the back row as either nonexistent, uninterested, impractical, or impotent. It then replaces God with one of their own making that fits how they want to live. It is as if they believe God, if He were only as smart as they, would have eventually arrived at the same conclusion.

In essence, such individuals have replaced God with themselves and, as their own new deity, create a belief system that fits the lifestyle or behavior they seek to justify. Unfortunately, the resulting pop-culture patchwork rarely stands the test of time, nor has it developed the necessary foundation to endure the sudden, severe trials of life. It certainly breaks down when applied to a blended-family situation. It is comparable to the unwise little pigs that built their houses of straw or sticks. When you make yourself the God of your world, it may work during the bright sun of noonday. But it tends to fall apart when the wolf stands at the door.

Service Confirms the Foundation

The worst phrase that can be uttered in our family is, "I don't care!" Our children know that if one doesn't care, then little of value can be accomplished. In addition, if they don't care about someone else, why should they expect others to care about them? It is not enough to lecture them on caring. That is a *what* discussion. Words may have their place but rarely work alone. It is actions that set examples, provide experience, and give us the opportunity to make a difference. Then a constructive *why* discussion is more meaningful.

In that context, it is important to incorporate service as part of your blended family values. There are endless opportunities to serve. But in the case of a blended family, ways must be found to do it together. There are opportunities available in the home, with extended family members, in the community, at school, in the neighborhood, within church congregations, or elsewhere.

Giving service together as a family can be a great partner in reinforcing a caring, compassionate belief system. There is a miracle that happens between family members as they serve. It could be as simple as shoveling an elderly neighbor's walks after a heavy snowfall or visiting those in the hospital or shut-ins. Leah and our teenage daughter have deep cleaned in homes after neighbors have had babies, been ill, have been in the process of moving, or undergone operations. We have helped people move, weed, repair, plant, and clean. Teaching a family to focus on filling another's need builds their ability to identify and respond to others on their own.

A few years ago we had a destructive windstorm in our city. Sustained hurricane-force winds, in excess of one hundred miles per hour, knocked over thousands of large trees and damaged countless homes and properties. We participated with literally thousands of others in the cleanup, which took many days after the severe storm. It was an uplifting experience for the entire community, and we treasured the opportunity to be involved as a family.

There is another benefit of service that must be included. It teaches children they can accomplish hard things. Life is full of difficult paths to achieve objectives. Graduating from high school, college, or graduate school is tough. Landing the right job and getting on the path to a solid career is another. Being a good spouse can be both trying and critical to happiness. Raising children is a challenge that never ends although it also never stops bringing joy. Serving together as a family teaches children that they can thrive in difficult situations. It teaches them why the hard times can also be the best times because that is when they grow the most. Such lessons are best learned in the trenches; there is no academic substitution.

Our children are growing up in a world that worships convenience—where many are unwilling to go out of their way for another. Teenagers in particular are naturally drawn toward their own inward focus. Life is too often absorbed by school, friends, homework, sports, or other personal activities and interests. Unless parents structure service into the family framework, this becomes all they know. Thus even a healthy family can unintentionally enable in their children a sense of entitlement and self-focus.

Successful families seek opportunities to serve individually because it is part of their family belief system. It is who they are and helps them with who they are becoming. Together we have discovered that compassionate service is best given on another's doorstep. What we mean by this is that you are best able to serve and connect by going into other people's lives rather than by requiring them to come into yours.

We recall a weekend when two of our college-age sons noticed a neighbor prepping and sodding his yard. They had other plans, but without a word they spontaneously decided to lend a hand. It was gratifying to discover later their kind act of service. When your children begin to spontaneously look to serve others, you know the family belief system is gaining traction.

Having a basic cornerstone of values that help blended family members look beyond the fearsome *what* to a true understanding of *why* and then problem solve the *how* makes all the other principles easier to apply.

This foundation must be based on truth and lived every day. It must also have practical application. Further, that belief system must be tested and proven by each member. Service toward others cements this process through action. It allows compassion to be experienced first-hand as family members learn that they can do hard things. A family that builds upon this solid cornerstone will find more joy in their home and greater satisfaction in their lives. It becomes the backbone of a blended family thus allowing it to effectively bear burdens and endure trials.

CHAPTER X

Principle #9: Listening to Understand

Everyone has a Story

Life can become an endless stream of second-guessing when you find yourself unexpectedly single with children. Self-doubt regarding worth and purpose are common questions, especially when divorce is involved. We dislike the term *broken family* when describing a divorce. It is not only demeaning to the parents, but it has negative implications for each family member. We have met many wonderful men, women, and children who are left to reorient their lives in the wake of death or divorce. They struggle for various periods, but this does not diminish the fact that they are fantastic and valuable people. They are certainly not broken.

Sometimes as single parents or blended families work through the issues that arise as part of their disrupted lives, it is helpful to seek outside assistance. Such guidance can come from friends, family, ministers, professional counseling services, and prayer. Some or all of these resources may be vital as lives are reconstructed. Professional, experienced counselors can be a helpful part of the process as individuals and families attempt to move forward. Seeking available help does not make one less of a person.

Clark remembers, after passing through a difficult period as an older teenager, he had an opportunity to sit with an inspiring religious leader. While he felt good about his decisions to overcome challenging circumstances, his confidence had been badly shaken. It did not help that when he looked at people around him, they all seemed so perfect. He had yet to learn that every person has a story. It is that personal story—good and bad—that gives them understanding, perspective, and wisdom if they make good choices along the way. Even bad choices can be overcome by subsequent good choices.

Clark described his feeling of inadequacy and his concern about ever being whole. This great religious man listened quietly. As their conversation drew to a close, he provided a nugget of wisdom that remains important over forty years later. He explained that difficult experiences happen to everyone. Sometimes these can push us to the edge of our ability to cope. But we are never alone in these trials. A loving heavenly Father is always there to support and lighten our burdens so we can endure. Then one day we find ourselves in a position to provide counsel to another who is in the depths of their own similar trial. Our experiences will then allow us to provide compassionate help, love, and most of all hope.

And so it has been with both of us. Our most challenging experiences have allowed us to hear the cries of our children and others when they come. It has allowed us to draw upon experiences and, with guidance from the Holy Spirit, provide comfort, strength, and hope.

Empowerment Thinking

More than one of our children has benefitted from the full spectrum of previously referenced guidance. It is just as important to know what is *not* the issue as it is to know what the issue is. But any type of counseling resource, whether formal or informal, is of little use if the individual is unwilling to be open and honest with themselves. It requires a special kind of courage to consider the full range of personal responsibility. It can be a difficult and humbling process. But it is also ultimately cleansing and empowering.

Taking responsibility for our actions and our occasional failings even if sometimes blame could be spread around is a powerful act. Fully acknowledging what part of any situation you had or could have had influence over is tremendously enlightening. Learning to apply this type of thinking to life's challenges can occasionally be embarrassing or humbling. However, as we decide to take responsibility and deal with related consequences we also engage in problem solving and self-empowerment.

Over time and with practice we learn that no matter how bad the situation is we have the power to change or overcome. Perhaps more importantly through this process we also teach ourselves that we have the power to avoid similar problems in the future. Why? Because we are not helpless. We can make better choices. We can learn from our experiences and through doing so we become stronger, better, and more successful at living life.

It becomes an incredibly empowering experience that both cleanses the soul and allows a person to begin moving forward again. This fearless approach to self-evaluation is a sure path to betterment. It can determine whether one will create a new life from ashes and pain or wallow for years in backward-looking victimization.

Listen to a Higher Source

As observers, we must be patient and allow each individual to make progress on their own, even if it is only discovering their need to progress. There was a morning when Clark entered the garage from our kitchen. After putting up the electric garage door, he heard something in the rafters. He first thought it might be a bat for all its banging around. But it turned out to be a large robin. It had apparently flown in the evening before. The bird was unable to get out of the garage even though the main door was wide open. It instinctively kept trying to fly upward, an effort that resulted in a thump against the ceiling and the bird returning to rest upon the top of the open garage door. Clark used a walking stick to try to guide the bird down and out of the garage. Several minutes of trying to coax the bird onto the stick were fruitless. Its raw instincts prevented it from understanding that to be free and fly upward, it had to first fly down. Finally, purely by chance, the bird fell from its perch and began its flight at a low enough level that took it out of the garage.

Both parents and children in blended families must learn the same lesson. All too often we ignore those around us who are attempting to guide us to more stable footing in our lives. We pursue our own will and figuratively bang our heads against the ceiling again and again in a futile attempt to gain freedom. The path forward may have been there, but too often we look in the wrong places. Then finally, out of exhaustion or perhaps by chance, we discover what others have been trying to show us all along. Always being there for our children cannot solve the problem by itself. They need to learn to submit their will to the guidance of others enough to be educated in a better way. This type of learning cannot be dictated. We must be patient. It may be necessary to watch them flail around for extended periods. But they will eventually open up even if it is only because they are tired of banging their heads against the wall. Be ready when that quality moment arrives, and a powerful bond will be born.

Many years ago one of our preteen sons was struggling. An outside professional was engaged to help. An interesting realization occurred during one of the sessions. The wisdom of the counselor in that moment has been passed on to others in various appropriate situations over the years.

The session was challenging as we tried to address the severe confusion our son was having as he attempted to balance conflicting loyalties, aggressive behavior, and parental campaigning. There was some difficult back and forth discussion. Finally, he blurted out, "You don't listen!" in anguish and obvious pain. There was a silent moment and an internal prayerful struggle. The counselor's response enlightened like a ray of sunshine on a dark cloudy day. Her counsel was essentially, "Because a person disagrees with you doesn't mean they didn't listen or understand what you said."

This is tough counsel, but as we have frequently learned, it is also insightful. When a person claims another is not listening, it can be a way to shut down the conversation, sidestep responsibility, and continue to assert that their position is correct when it may not be. We have tried to emphasize this with our children. We certainly are not perfect but always try to listen and understand in our family. That does not automatically mean that agreement is the result.

It is also possible, and we have made this mistake, that a parent fails to actively listen to a child or their spouse. Because of this we often do hear the wrong message and not understand what the other person is saying. The key is not whether you agree or disagree. It is whether you engage in listening and asking questions until you understand. Only by understanding who you are communicating with, and why, do you earn the right to respond. This is true on both sides of the conversation. Sometimes we get so involved in telling the story, thinking through our next response, or blindly seeking a particular outcome, that we misunderstand. Such behavior defeats the point of communicating in the first place.

Causes of Miscommunication

Blended families can have additional issues that overlay all communication. These can create tension, fragile interaction, and false expectations regarding predisposed reactions that are not reality. Countless volumes have been written on the subject of effective communication. Our goal here is to provide some ideas regarding how we have wrestled this alligator in our blended family.

Miscommunication in our family most often occurs when the following circumstances are present:

1. We are more interested in formulating our next response than listening to what is being said.

2. We voice our comment or statement then cut off responses by saying we don't want to talk about it or by walking away or shutting the door. We call this *shutting down* the conversation or person.

3. We are distracted by other thoughts or activities and don't pay close enough attention.

4. We prejudge or anticipate certain responses that are not, in fact, reality.

5. We have pre-formulated opinions and jump in with a quick answer or talk over the other person before we know what was going to be said.

6. We try to fix the problem when all the person wants is someone to listen.

7. We fail to ask enough questions to clarify what is being communicated.

8. We convey our thoughts or responses in words or a tone that causes a defensive reaction rather than promoting listening.

9. We read things into the conversation that are not intended.

10. We are impatient and try to rush the conversation.

11. We commandeer the conversation, inadvertently robbing them of title to their own thinking and problem-solving process.

12. We internally demean the intelligence or worth of the speaker thereby giving ourselves permission to ignore what is said.

The point is that there are numerous ways to shut down or promote communication. Leah has a gift for drawing the true feelings out of our children in their own comfort zone. She can seamlessly slide back and forth between right-brained general creative communication and left-brained specific task and schedule-oriented communication. Clark possesses the ability to communicate on different levels as well, but usually he must make a conscious decision regarding the general and specific discussions.

We have children of both types in our blended family. Some tend toward the artistic and chafe when they have structure, schedules, or study plans that need to be addressed in specific. Others will immediately organize the schedule with times and objectives. Both types can then fail to think outside the box, frequently setting themselves up for unexpected head banging and frontal assaults when sudden change occurs.

In addition, our children's approach to life can bounce back and forth, depending on situational demands. As a result, our blended family communication has required us to develop nimble and flexible strategies. We manage the delicate balance through actively listening and understanding. We must walk that fine line and not irritate a child by pushing for too many specifics when they think they are done with the conversation. There will always be another opportunity to reinforce a point. On the other hand, we cannot back off too early without raising questions they at least need to think about.

We have previously discussed the value of showing your children and spouse respect. Listening to understand naturally demonstrates that respect. Children must know that you appreciate where they are coming from, respect their position, and value their thoughts. In doing so, parents are more likely to find that children will listen to their advice. Most of what we have discussed is common sense that can be patiently and effectively employed in relationships. However, there are outside distractions that can severely challenge a blended family's ability to communicate.

Distractions Hinder Communication

We live in a world constantly connected through smart devices. One-hundred years ago if you wanted to speak to someone who was not in your presence, you had three choices. You traveled to visit them, wrote them a letter, or sent them a telegram. Later, with the advent of the telephone, you could make a call. Even more recently, you could send them an email from your desktop computer.

Each of these required a special effort to be in a specific place and probably with at least a partially thought-through purpose. Today is the era of cell phones, smartphones, and full electronic connection. With little or no forethought, we text, chat, and insta-everything. Partial thoughts or fragments of interaction seem to be the rule rather than the exception.

Our children frequently text with friends for hours to communicate simple plans. We have asked, "Why don't you just make a phone call and resolve it in a two-minute conversation?" One response we have received to this question has intrigued us. It usually goes something like, "When I text, I don't have to respond in real time. I can think about my response before I make it." Now that makes sense, although it does little to help their real-time communication skills.

Our teenage daughter is a smartphone pro. Her thumbs are blindingly fast. But she is also respectful of family time and turns it off or puts it away when it is time for face-to-face interaction. She realizes there are circumstances when there is no effective substitute for communicating in person.

Although on one occasion she responded defensively to one of our questions. We were driving her and a friend to an activity. They were sitting in the back seat. They ignored each other while instead constantly texting third parties. We thought this was impolite and let her know after the friend activity ended. She responded, "You don't understand the modern world. Young people don't need to talk to each other when they're together. It's okay to be talking to everyone else."

We were stunned. Of course, personal interaction has always been, continues to be, and will always be important in personal and family relations. Certainly, being polite and actually being with the person you are with is important also. This was a misunderstanding about the world that could not be allowed to stand. However, nothing would be accomplished in that moment, so we allowed it to pass unchallenged, filing it away for a later time.

An appropriate teaching moment came a few days later. Our daughter had a few friends over for a get-together and we provided the pizza. We were honored to be invited to sit with them while they ate. There were various smartphone interruptions, which reminded us of our earlier conversation. We inquired if we could ask the group something on a current social topic. We indicated their opinions would be greatly appreciated. They enthusiastically agreed. The responses were interesting because it was a mixed group of boys and girls. The conversation went like this:

"Do your parents or your older siblings have smartphones?" We made it clear that in reference to older siblings we were primarily referring to married siblings.

"Yes," all agreed.

"Do they know how to use them? Can they text, chat, Facebook, Tweet, email and do other normal things online with their devices?"

There was some chuckling, but the answer was a qualified and slightly sarcastic, "Yes."

"Do your parents and older siblings have friends?"

"Yes." This was kind of a "Duh, of course," response.

"Do you think they have more friends in the world than you do?"

There was some conversation on this point, but since those we were referring to had been alive longer and had generally been more places, worked, or gone to college, etc., the answer was again, "Yes."

"When your parents or married siblings are together, do they spend the majority of their time on their phones communicating with other people?"

"No, they talk to each other," was the consensus.

Then came the critical question that we worried might feel like a trap.

"Why do they talk to each other when they are together instead of using their phones to communicate with others?"

There was an uncomfortable silence as the discussion's implications sunk in. One of the boys answered profoundly, "Because they care about each other."

The others nodded in agreement.

Wow, what an awesome answer! Some teaching moments just happen. We let him know that he was exactly right and asked, "Shouldn't we want anyone we are spending time with to also know we care about them?"

They agreed, and our daughter's eyes sparkled letting us know she had made a mental connection with the previous conversation. The lesson was more powerful because they participated in getting there instead of simply being told. There are few things more important than actually being present with the person you are with. That doesn't mean there can never be an interruption or an important call. But the constant noise level of selfies, texting, earbuds, apps, and Snapchat is so loud when our children are with others, including family members, that it is as if they are not present at all.

Give the Gift of Attention

This is particularly important with parent-child interactions. It is an honor to have a child approach you and open a door to allow you to see into their life. Set aside what you are doing and give them your whole attention. The decision to really listen may be the most important part of your conversation. Whether they are asking for something, sharing a great moment from their day, or venting about a challenge, you have already set the proper course. You have told them they are important to you—that they have value and are loved. What greater message can a parent send to a son or daughter?

There is no better way to build relationships in a blended family than taking time to listen to and understand what your children have to say. Whether the time for discussion or solutions comes immediately, later, or not at all is less important. Respect will grow. Kindness and love will be exhibited. Lessons will be learned by all, and a base for further communication will be broadened.

Then, with patience, more conversations will occur and healing, if necessary, will take place. Teaching a child the value of listening to understand is like teaching a child the value of reading to comprehend. Learning to enjoy reading is the basic educational building block. Children will be more successful in all their subjects if they improve reading comprehension. After all, every subject has its foundation in reading.

In a like manner, good communication skills are the basis for all life interactions. The art of listening to understand is the foundation of all communication. It is almost never about what you think you have to say; rather, it is usually about what you can learn. That happens through listening.

Principle #10: We Love to Laugh

The Healing Properties of Humor

In the popular 1960s movie *Mary Poppins*, Bert the chimney sweep takes Mary Poppins and the Banks children to visit Uncle Albert, played superbly by comedian Ed Wynn. A concerned Mary is told that Uncle Albert has developed an apparently serious condition. They arrive to find him floating near the ceiling in a state of laughing euphoria. This rare malady is apparently caused by being overly happy. The resulting laughter causes anyone afflicted to float uncontrollably. Uncle Albert sings a song to explain the source of his problem titled, "I Love to Laugh." Soon all feel the effect and float up to have tea at the ceiling. Mary Poppins saves the day by reminding them of sad things, which literally brings them back to earth.

There are few behaviors as uplifting as laughter. Medical studies have a long history of describing the positive health impacts. Researchers are unsure whether it is the laughter itself that makes people feel better or the traits that often accompany it like a good sense of humor, positive attitude, or the support of friends and family.

When a person laughs, they stretch muscles throughout their face and body. Pulse and blood pressure go up, and they breathe faster thus oxygenating their blood. These are the same effects as a mild workout. While this does not replace exercise, a recent Johns Hopkins study indicated that a good laugh can boost the immune system and have a positive effect on memory and mental performance.

Our blended family has discovered that a sense of humor, even if it is a bit cheesy, can be an important contributor to a healthy, happy home. Our children are mostly adults now. They have their own lives, activities, and involvement. Yet we still get together whenever we can.

We had two of our single sons over for dinner during the writing of this chapter and decided to play games afterward. We never got to the games. Why? Things happen, particularly funny things. After clearing the table and finishing the dishes, our sons and teenage daughter sat talking on the living room couch. Suddenly, we heard raucous laughter and inquired as to what was going on. They held up their phones simultaneously in reply.

All three had downloaded the same photo app. It allowed them to take a selfie, and the app would radically distort their looks like a carnival fun house curved mirror. These pictures created the most humorous and unusual distortions that made them look like cartoon characters. They could even add cartoon features. We joined the insanity and took our turn being horribly distorted. We laughed until our heads and sides hurt. Is this what it feels like to have a laughter workout? If it does indeed boost our immune systems, we might have been invincible for the rest of the evening.

Spontaneous and Unexpected

We enjoy regular date time with adult children and grandchildren on evenings out to local restaurants or participating in other activities. We like to cultivate a quick wit and personally believe it may help stave off old age. Even something as simple as making a reservation can have its humorous moments if you love the way the English language works. The young lady taking phone reservations innocently asked, "How large is your party?"

Clark's response caught her by surprise, "Oh, we're all about average size."

After regaining her composure, she asked, "Will you be needing a booster seat or a high chair?"

This was too big an opportunity to pass up. He looked at Leah and the surrounding children and then said, "Thank you for asking, but I haven't used one of those for several years."

We sometimes have fun with the menu when we order if we sense the server is particularly good humored. One restaurant had a dish called smothered chicken, which meant it had gravy poured over the chicken. Leah ordered it, then Clark looked seriously at the server and asked, "Can you tell us please if the chicken was humanely smothered?" We all cracked up, including the server. On another occasion after ordering a steak, the server asked Clark which side dishes he would like by using verbal shorthand, "Two sides?" Clark's straight-faced response, "Yes, I'd like it cooked on both sides," certainly livened up the order.

Sometimes we catch the server by surprise. Leah usually will ask when ordering fish if it is farmed or wild caught. She did and ordered the wild-caught salmon at one restaurant. At another we asked the server if the chicken was farmed or wild.

The server was stumped and said, "I don't know. I'll have to ask the manager."

We let her in on the little joke and all laughed although she did point out that it would have been fair game to inquire if it was free-range chicken. We were relieved. It might be a little scary to come unexpectedly upon a wild chicken. Having fun as a family should be spontaneous and uplifting. In our case it can happen at any time, without warning. We sometimes feel like Inspector Clouseau and his faithful assistant Cato in the 1964 Pink Panther film, *A Shot in the Dark*. In order to keep his skills sharp, the Inspector instructed Cato to attack him at any moment, also without warning.

Our lives are not immune from dealing with difficulties. We have known sickness, death, disappointment, sorrow, and discouragement. But our home is also a happy place. We love to laugh. A good sense of humor is welcome, and a solid pun is always appreciated even if cringe-worthy. This, combined with unconditional love, has made our home a welcoming place appreciated by our children, grandchildren, and their friends.

What is Humor?

To have a truly happy, rather than a counterfeit happy, atmosphere, parents must teach their children by word and example the nature of true humor. Our society, movies, and media are full of counterfeit, demeaning substitutes that masquerade as humor. Healthy humor is not found in the telling of a dirty or demeaning joke or story, nor is it found in destructive gossip, foul language, or crudeness. Media is full of such things. They tear down our spirits and pollute the atmosphere around all who hear or see it. These counterfeits push positive feelings and light aside while filling the home with heavy, oppressive darkness. We feel the darkness at the edges of our minds just discussing it in this chapter. But this principle is about what works, lifts, and heals rather than cheap counterfeits.

One does not have to look too far in our blended family for good humor. It just happens. When one of our grandsons was four, Clark had one of those spontaneous moments while picking him up from school. The conversation started innocently:

"What did you do in school today?"

"We are learning about dinosaurs."

"Oh really, I love dinosaurs. What is your favorite one?"

"Tyrannosaurus Rex."

"That's one of my favorites too."

"They're extinct. But you wouldn't know that because you're not a paleontologist."

Clark struggled to stifle a giggle here because it was so humorous to hear our little grandson use a word that was longer than he was tall. Somehow, he kept his composure because it was clear our grandson was serious about his new knowledge. The conversation continued:

"What do you like most about the T-Rex?"

"They have really long sharp teeth. They are longer than your hand."

"That sounds dangerous. Maybe it's good they are extinct." Showing off his knowledge on the subject to appear cool Clark added, "Didn't they have little short arms also?"

"Yes."

"How could they reach their teeth to brush them?"

His immediate response was disarming, "They couldn't; that's why they went extinct."

It is unexpected quality moments like this that so often enrich our lives and bring us closer together. In addition,

Grandpa learned something new. He never realized that T-Rex dinosaurs were extinct because their arms were not long enough to engage in proper oral hygiene.

Life is full of humorous situations and fun moments that are not at the expense of anyone. It is important to promote raising standards of humor. Blended families must be vigilant regarding the kind of media that is allowed to air within the home. Movies, downloaded videos, television shows, music, and the like should be carefully filtered to eliminate dark, crude, offensive, and demeaning material. It is not enough just to eliminate the bad. We must be vigilant to ensure that our home is filled with things that uplift and encourage. Establishing such standards requires involvement of every family member so that all may take title to living by the standards set.

Of course, we do not leave our standards in the parlor when we step outside. We take them with us when attending events and activities. Inappropriate humor is akin to mud on our shoes. We track it everywhere we go. For example, there are family-oriented websites that we utilize to determine the appropriateness of any movie before deciding whether it should be viewed. Motion picture ratings are simply insufficient. The truth is that there are many options for fun activities and entertainment that will uplift and edify. It may take a few extra minutes to double-check, but it is worth it.

Avoiding Burnout

Clark worked in the investment banking and corporate finance industries for many years. These are high-pressure, high-performance workplaces where employee burnout is a regular occurrence. Competitiveness often replaces friendship and cheerfulness, and compassion can be easily set aside in favor of passion and intensity.

Most in these professions are intellectually driven. However, too many fall into the trap of taking themselves and every circumstance way too seriously. The result is frequent illness or employee bailout due to stress and performance pressure. Clark survived and thrived through countless highly stressful periods for over thirty-five years using the following strategies:

1. Keeping spiritual and emotional sides nourished and well grounded
2. Maintaining a good sense of humor
3. Keeping priorities on home and family
4. Balancing work with outside interests including vigorous physical, service, and spiritual activities
5. Generally not taking himself or his work too seriously

At the end of the day, it was a valuable and stimulating career where an individual could impact many for good. It was also just a series of jobs, and he never allowed them to define who he was.

A few years ago, a son and daughter-in-law introduced us to a board game named *Quelf.* The board consists of a path of different-colored squares that circle around from start to finish. Depending on the color of the square, the player must pick a card and follow its directions. The card may require the player to answer a question, perform a role or skit, obey a humorous rule until the rule changes or the game is over, demonstrate a talent, or simply do something unusual. It is all in good taste and is a fun icebreaker. We enjoy playing it as a family and especially introducing it when our children bring friends or dates over to meet the family.

Sometimes the individual cannot tell anyone what the card requires them to do. The other players must figure it out. We had a couple over one evening. The husband drew a card that told him to get up without saying anything, walk to the bathroom, close the door, and stay there until someone came and looked for him.

We did not think anything of it when he got up and went to the bathroom. His turn was over, so we continued the game. He didn't return, of course. It got back around to him and he was still missing. We wondered what might be taking so long. We called to him, but he was not allowed to answer based on the card's direction. Finally, Leah went to look for him and discovered the cause. Laughter reverberated around the room.

It isn't just laughter that uplifts a blended family. It is a positive atmosphere and happy environment that reassures each family member that they are part of something good. It promotes a welcome feeling where they feel safe.

See Through Another's Eyes

Some time ago one of our daughters had her hair cut. It was not a big deal. She simply had a trim to clean up split ends. But it was a huge event to her, and she felt her hair looked very different. Leah went with her, advised her during the process, and then gave her positive reinforcement afterward. Leah let Clark know of the important event in her life, so he could answer correctly when the test came. "Do you notice anything different, Dad?" It was in fact noticeable and nice. Our responses helped her feel good about what, for her, was a potentially traumatic decision.

Even traumatic family moments can have a funny, uplifting twist. On another occasion, one of our daughters had reached that awkward time as a near-teenager. She still liked younger activities but felt the tug to be more grown up. This particular daughter has always planned for things way too far ahead of time.

In this situation she had mail ordered a Halloween costume eight weeks before Halloween. It arrived on an evening in early October. That particular evening we were in a rush to get to an important event that required us to be on time. It was a Disney-style Pocahontas outfit. Twenty minutes before we had to leave, she decided to try on the costume. It fit well enough so that with a little tailoring she would look very authentic. She stood looking in the mirror and burst into tears. It took several minutes to get out of her what was wrong. Her tear-streaked face looked up and she said, "I look like Pocahontas."

"Yes, that's what the costume is supposed to be," Leah said.

She burst into tears again. "But I look like a child!"

Suddenly, we realized that her immediate goal had changed since she ordered the outfit. This was a moment of crisis and could upset the entire evening. Clark said a brief, private, please-help-us-deal-with-this prayer and had a flash of inspiration. He immediately responded, "I don't think you look like Pocahontas."

She gave him a confused look.

He continued. "You look more like…Sacagawea."

There was a pause. She gazed critically at the mirror. A light came into her eyes and she immediately calmed down. Without looking away from the mirror she said in a calm, collected voice, "Yeah…I can do Sacagawea. That'll work."

Somehow being Sacagawea made her feel more grown up. Some mysteries are beyond understanding. We were relieved and got in the car on time. But the punch line came unexpectedly about ten minutes later. She had recovered from her meltdown when Clark said, "Back at the house before we left, what was that all about?"

Her one-word answer threw us into a side-splitting laugh attack.

The back seat was completely quiet for a moment before she responded with a deadpan expression: "Hormones."

We realized that there was no better or more complete answer. She had delivered a sermon with one word. The entire episode has become part of our cherished family history.

She was self-aware enough to recognize her moment for exactly what it was. This was directly related to the effectiveness of the conversations Leah had engaged in with her as she approached and began dealing with her physical changes.

Leah has taken time to teach our children that life is full of moments when we may be in pain, discomfort, inconvenienced, or some other physical, emotional, or spiritual difficulty. She has explained that we must work hard to keep such challenges from leaking into our interactions with others. No matter the pain or difficulty, a kind word, even if it is a warning, is always the best course. Leah's efforts in this case demonstrate the value of providing anticipatory counsel. Of course, that is not always possible, but in this case it worked beautifully.

Many years ago Clark remembers one of his bio-daughters sitting in church at the tender age of four. Someone was giving a talk from the pulpit, relating a tender and heartfelt experience. The atmosphere was quiet and reverent. This particular daughter had always had the most interesting thoughts, and she was drawing to keep herself occupied. She turned to Clark and showed him the picture. He tried to interpret it and could tell it was some kind of figure. He whispered, "That's very good. Can you tell me about it?"

She responded, "That's you, Daddy."

He was touched and proud, nodding his head in approval.

Then she looked seriously at the picture and seemed to study it intently for a few moments.

Turning back to her dad, she shook her head and said, "No, it's a turkey."

It was very difficult to stifle the resulting laughter, and I'm sure we disrupted the meeting. However, both may be true. Dad is sometimes a turkey.

Creativity

Being creative is an important part of developing uplifting relationships. As part of this we naturally discover new adventures and personal connectors that tie us to each child or grandchild. Our grandchildren look forward to Grandpa's *zoomps* when they visit. Before describing what *zoomps* are, some background is necessary. We have taught our children and grandchildren that a kiss on the cheek never stays on the cheek. It immediately absorbs into the skin and travels straight to the heart where it lands with a *zoomp* sound. This is always accompanied by a pat on one's chest to confirm its arrival.

This journey must be assisted by the one receiving the kiss on the cheek rubbing it in. This all started when one of us was given a wet sticky kiss and rubbed our cheek. Our daughter noticed and asked if we were rubbing it off. Our answer has always been that we rub it in, not off.

When it is time to go, Grandpa picks up the grandkids and kisses them on the cheek, then they kiss Grandpa on the cheek. Both participants rub their cheek to start the process and then pat their own chests, confirming the arrival of the kiss at the heart and say together in a loud voice, *"Zoomp!"* It can be quite theatrical and is always accompanied with a big smile. We laughed one day when a son and daughter-in-law related a story about their one-year-old son. He had walked around the house all week practicing his *zoomps* and patting his chest. The next time they visited, he would not leave without his first *zoomp*. He executed it perfectly, of course, due to all the practice.

Sometimes our children acquire pet names as part of our cheerful attempt at mixing humor with improvement advice. Our teenage daughter is a good example. She is easily distracted. She might start toward her room to get ready for bed or do homework and have her attention diverted along the way by almost anything shiny. A thought, a text, a piece of hair out of place, or a new idea about a line in a song she might be working on.

After seeing the Disney movie *UP* we coined a nickname for her. You will remember the dog Dug they find living in the wilderness. He has a device on his neck that allows him to speak. However, he is constantly distracted mid-thought or mid-sentence. He would cock his head and say, "Squirrel." So our daughter's affectionate nickname is Squirrel. It always brings a smile and frequently is the tool we use to remind her that she actually went upstairs with the intent of doing something else.

The Squirrel concept isn't just a nickname, it's a strategy. Yes, it's a strategy in dealing effectively and positively with difficult or emotional childhood moments. We have had days with many of our children at all ages when we ask how life is going.

Occasionally, the response comes back that it's been a very terrible, horrible day. At other times, one of our children or grandchildren seems hopelessly upset or in the process of a complete meltdown. The first thing we try to remember is to listen and avoid the frontal assault. Frontal assaults involve blasting them about *what* they did wrong and dictating *how* to fix it. Telling them they need to grow up and deal with it before we fully understand the *why* never improves the situation. In fact, it often produces arguments, anger, and piles on new stress.

We use the revised and adapted *Squirrel* approach. It usually works even when they are older and know exactly what we are doing. A child who doesn't want to go to bed can have their perspective changed if they are not going up for the purpose of going to sleep. Instead they get to go up to read a book or be told one of the family's made-up stories like *Ollie the Octopus*, *Teeny-Tiny Princess*, or *Brave Howie*. A good story is a great distraction to get through the moment. By the time the issue resurfaces, their attitude is changed or they have already fallen asleep.

We also read books together. In the case of one of our sons who did not like to read as a preteen, it became his special time with a parent. At the same time, he began to appreciate the wonderful adventures and places to which a book could carry him. As a result, he developed a real interest in reading that continues to bless his life.

Allowing children to talk it out while you actively listen can be positive as well. However, in other situations simply focusing their attention on something else works immediately. Give them something new to act out on the stage of their mind. By doing so, you replace part or all of the current difficulty.

We have used a walk outside, a question about an unrelated but interesting matter, a request for assistance, a request for ideas about something the parent is dealing with, or simply refocusing them on another toy or thought. The latter approach is especially useful with young children when they are having disagreements over who gets to play with a particular toy. It may help if you remove the toy that is the focus of the disagreement and redirect both children toward another activity or object.

The lesson can later be taught about the importance of sharing. The *Squirrel* approach is not meant to avoid teaching opportunities. It is designed to get through the moment and maintain a positive spirit and atmosphere. Sometimes it doesn't matter how good a teacher the parent may be. The child or adult will not and cannot effectively absorb a lesson when it is competing with contention, anger, raised voices, or argument.

As we mature, the *Squirrel* strategy often develops into healthy stress-relieving behavior. It can take the form of exercise, playing a musical instrument, reading a good book, or going on a ride or walk. Regardless of the outlet, we all have times when we need to unwind.

Music and a Healthy Environment

Members of a blended family experience all the usual problems of work, social involvement, and school. In addition, they also face seemingly insurmountable extra burdens. Regular moves back and forth between bio-parent homes, loyalty conflicts, parental acting out, anger, confusion, bitterness, self-doubt, rejection, bullying, the general tumult of divorce, fending for themselves with absentee parents, single-parent family challenges, or blending new families can all tip the scales.

Having healthy, safe relationships, activities, and calming interests allow us all to survive the moment and regain proper perspective. There will always be time to re-approach the situation with a fresh perspective and attitude.

Positive and uplifting music is another resource that can make a difference in lightening the atmosphere. There was a day one of those, "I can't do this anymore!" calls came from one of the children. You know the phase in life that can involve some or all of the following: newly married, both working, going to college, a first baby in the home. There are few times in life when the stress level is higher, and society seems to expect them to handle it all with no experience.

Following this call, Clark drove from work to the apartment with no clear idea of how to help. All he knew was that the Spirit told him he needed to visit. The drive took about twenty minutes and he struggled, praying to know how to handle the situation. Then he felt further inspiration guide the way. The thought came to him to have them sing an uplifting song. The name of the song also surfaced in his mind. It was a sung by pioneers to raise their spirits during the long nineteenth-century westward trek.

He knocked on the door and was invited in. The home was heavy with tension. He asked if they had a hymn book, which they produced, and he said, "Let's sing!" They had expected a lecture or counsel, so they looked at him as if he were speaking a foreign language. He suggested again that they sing and so they did, reluctantly at first. They stumbled and mumbled through the first verse but continued until they had completed all four verses. The atmosphere had dramatically improved, but not enough, so they sang the hymn again.

The second time through, they sang with growing feeling and gusto. By the time they had completed the hymn a second time, the atmosphere had completely changed. It was positive and uplifting.

Clark counseled them to keep the book handy and use it whenever they felt tension building. He promised to follow-up and ask them regularly how many hymns it took to get through the day, knowing if it was a five- or ten-hymn day, it was probably a tough one, but if it was a one hymn day, things were pretty good. They remain together years later although probably, like the rest of us, still singing from time to time.

This chapter contains nuggets that will benefit every family. However, due to the additional burdens borne by blended families, a good laugh, well-timed and sincere smile, word of encouragement, act of kindness, strategic distraction, or uplifting song can make a positive difference. Always leave time to enjoy the moments and smile at the beautiful view. Life is wonderful, exceptional, and amazing. A little humor brings light, and light always dispels the darkness. It allows family members to break from the stress of the day and be reminded of the more important things in life. We like to have fun, and we do. It's become part of our blended family DNA.

Chapter XII

Why the Principles Matter: Surviving Storms and Tragedy

The Principles Are Interconnected

In the previous chapters, we outlined principles our blended family uses to achieve successful outcomes. The blending process will go on for the rest of our lives, and we still have serious issues with which we are dealing. But an important pattern has been set. It is our hope, when we pass from this life, our children will carry on as a family without borders or labels. We view our family like any other. The fact that we are blended is more of an unconscious truth rather than a label that defines or limits.

These principles can have a powerful impact. Even families that only master one or two will be better off. However, we expect you have already noticed there is a secret sauce that binds. It is the realization that each of these principles works better when used in concert with the others. They are truly interdependent. Therefore, any effort to incorporate all ten principles will create a cross-supported structure increasing family stability and success.

That is why it is so difficult to address one principle without referencing the others. They interconnect to create a powerful interwoven fabric that even the most difficult trials cannot unravel.

Our trials have arrived in many forms. Some can be identified at a distance while others strike with little warning like a mountain storm. Some of these storms can be weathered with a little extra effort but others seem so overwhelming that we are left helpless to do anything but hang on and ride it out.

When the storm is already raging, it is too late to develop the behavior, traits, and resilience provided by these principles. They must be practiced, shared, and absorbed over time through consistent living. It is true that life can go on for months and sometimes years without a severe trial. These stretches tend to lull us into a state of complacency. During these pleasant stretches, it is easy to begin to believe that things will always be the same. Indeed, life's routine can take on a sameness that reinforces this illusion.

One day we awake to discover an incomprehensible event has occurred. The sudden reality dawns that nothing will ever be the same again. This is why these principles are so vital. They are lived, reinforced, and become embedded in who we are. Make them part of your family and you will be better prepared to face anything. Like the master black belt in karate, our reactions become instinctive and automatic. When terrible events occur, the principles and our belief system kick in immediately. Families who follow these principles will remain standing together, able to provide a healthy response. Examples of such events include death, job loss, economic collapse, illness, or a child acting out. We will briefly relate two personal family examples.

Storms and Answers Come

In February of 2017 one of our twenty-something sons informed us that he had been diagnosed with stage four Hodgkin's Lymphoma, cancer of the lymph system. He had nodes on his spine and numerous cancerous lymph glands and it had spread. It is impossible to express the devastating emotions we all shared. It was made worse because there was nothing we could do to help him overcome it. We could only be there and support his family through months of chemotherapy.

At times like this you fall back on your foundation, and prayer becomes an even more important part of your focus. Clark remembers a long night of such prayer and tears. Late in the night, a voice came to him as clear as day. It reminded him of the Savior's promise recorded in the Gospel of St. John that if we would follow Him and keep the commandments, He would give us a "Comforter … even the Spirit." Clark's mind calmed as he understood the Savior's promise that He "would not leave [us] comfortless." In that moment, he knew it would be all right in the end. We felt the Spirit with us through the entire process.

We adjusted to family life with chemotherapy as best we could. Halfway through the treatments, which were given every other week, we got a call explaining that the scheduled treatment was delayed because the doctors had to do some additional scans to check something out. No other detail was available. Our concern erupted in fears that the already severe stage had spread further. A horrific three-day delay occurred until the more detailed tests came back. We did what we could to carry on while living on the edge of this frightening abyss.

Clark remembers a moment when it all caught up with him. He was mowing the backyard lawn. The sun shone down on a beautiful spring day. Unexpectedly, a tidal wave broke. He felt his insides collapse, leaving him sobbing. His soul fled to its last redoubt and only solace of prayer. He next felt a warm rush of spiritual comfort that our son was not alone, and he would be all right. Two days later, news came back that was beyond belief. The formerly metastasized cancer was gone except for a couple of lymph glands that were shrunken and no longer hyper-metabolic. In other words, dormant.

Sometimes it is hard to recognize or understand an answer to a prayer. At other times, we chafe because the answer we get is not what we wanted. But an answer always comes. Once in a while, we are privileged to witness one of those Biblical-level miracles that are impossible to discount. However, through it all, we must find a way to remain standing as individuals and together as a family. Extreme stress can overcome all but the most dearly adhered-to belief systems. The question isn't whether a family has one, it is whether it is sufficiently part of their DNA to withstand the most terrible storms. Only principles that give us power to bear burdens, overcome, and make the divine real in our lives are worthy pursuits of a blended family.

Dealing with an Answer We Dread

There are times when, in spite of prayers, love, and faithfulness, a family is faced with a trial that ends in a way nobody wants. Leah's youngest sister was diagnosed with breast cancer some years ago. With operations and treatment, she improved, living a relatively normal life for a period of time. She was even able to have another child. More recently the cancer suddenly returned in the form of brain tumors. Further treatments were generally unsuccessful, and she finally elected to cease attempts to fight the disease. She went on home hospice to have a better quality of life for the limited time left. Leah and other family members were able to visit and comfort her and her family prior to her passing. It became a tender opportunity for closure and a time of heartfelt service.

During our marriage we, or our immediate family, have endured job disruptions; estranged children or other close family members; severe or chronic illness; sudden unexpected death or injury; and choices that our adult children occasionally make that we fear will lead to serious difficulty in life.

Terrible things happen to wonderful, loved people. Sometimes a resolution during this life does not occur. Such situations test a family's foundations in extraordinary ways. But a blended family that has grown together and developed interconnected principles can better rise to meet such challenges. They have each other to lean on when the dreaded answers come. It is absolutely true that you will not need all the tools in your toolbox every day. However, it is just as true that there will be days, weeks, and years when you will need every tool.

In conclusion, living these principles help a family blend and become truly unified. They will help to smooth the way, avoid or ease tensions, and create a home that is a safe harbor for each family member. It is important to understand that many combinations of beliefs, principles, values, and practices can achieve or nearly achieve that goal. The stronger and more committed the belief system, the stronger the family.

We have offered those principles that continue to work for us. However, there are times when everything you have and are as a family is pushed to the edge. Sometimes there is no shelter from the storm. In those cases, we can only hang on and pass through. These are the moments when an interwoven fabric of principles that have become part of who the family is may be the only thing that keeps it from flying to pieces. That is when a family discovers why such principles lived faithfully every day are so important. It is what motivated us to share them with you.

You are Good Enough – Bonus Principle

The challenge of blended-family life often pushes its members to the limits of their coping ability. During our fourteen years together, we have had many of these moments. We have previously discussed the importance of being on the same page—communication—having shared values and planning ahead from the very beginning, and other critical principles. Even when you do everything well and incorporate these principles effectively into your family, those days will still face you down. Whether it is serious illness, a child wandering on strange paths, estrangement with family members, difficulty with former spouses, or any of an infinite number of other issues, one final principle will help. Call it our bonus principle for any who has made it this far into the book. It is best illustrated by an example from the life of Jesus.

The Gospel of St. Mark relates the feeding of five-thousand-plus individuals who followed him into the desert. The Savior had compassion on them and taught them late into the day. Jesus' disciples suggested it was time to send the people away so they could find food for they had nothing to eat. Jesus was concerned they might faint along the way and asked his disciples to feed the multitude. They responded with a question suggesting that feeding the crowd might be extremely expensive and time consuming. Undeterred, the Savior asked the disciples to take an inventory of food the people had with them. They reported back that they found only five loaves and a few fishes, woefully insufficient to feed over five-thousand. The Savior took the meager offerings and broke them up in a basket, which was passed among the people who ate and were filled. Incredibly, Mark reports that twelve baskets of food were left over.

This is chronicled as one of the more stunning miracles Jesus performed during his life. But there is another message here. Jesus teaches all of us through the feeding of the five-thousand that if we give all we have, no matter how meager it may seem, *it will be enough.* He will fill the gap. We find this message's application especially meaningful to a blended family. It means that every parent and child in every family, including blended families, willing to put their faith and trust in the Lord can accomplish great things. It is not dependent on financial, spiritual, emotional, or physical prowess. It is certainly not limited by the lack thereof. Whatever each one of us has to give, if we are willing to give it all, will be enough.

We have struggled at times with children who don't seem to be able to move on and make an independent life for themselves. At other times we have strived with others haunted by depression or who obsess and dwell on past mistakes, shortcomings, or the unfairness of life. Give them your love, support, and make every effort to reach out and lift them up. Regardless of the outcome, you will know you did everything you could, and God will fill in the gap as His will is done. Teach them by your example that who they are and what they have can also be enough if they are willing to give. They too will see the gap filled. Sometimes this will involve friends, professionals, mentors, or unexpected people placed in your path. These are not coincidences. We have discovered that the divine hand often touches our lives through others. Do not give up.

So no matter the challenge you face in your blended family you are never alone in your effort. Giving all you can will be enough.

CHAPTER XIII

The Successful Blended Family

Act Early

We live in the high mountain valleys of the Rockies where winter includes frequent heavy snowfall. At over four-thousand feet above sea level, it is not uncommon for our community to get one or two feet of snow in single storms multiple times a season. This means snow shovels and snow blowers are well known in the community.

Snow has interesting properties. When it falls there are air pockets between each flake. This gives it that fluffy texture that makes it fun to ski and play in. We have learned that shoveling the driveway is easiest if done while the snow is freshly fallen. This means we clear the walks before moving our cars when possible because snow compresses as it settles, melts, or when weight is applied to it. As snow compresses, the air pockets are forced out. It then becomes heavier and more densely solid. Compressed, frozen, icy snow takes on the characteristics of concrete. While condensed snow makes a good snowman, snowball, ice fort, or snow cave, it becomes much more difficult, if not impossible, to shovel.

Difficulties in blended families have similar characteristics. Anticipating and avoiding problems, by employing the principles we've discussed, is always easier. However, when at-risk, distracted, or careless behavior becomes entrenched, it is difficult to reverse. Parents must then exercise patience until a thaw occurs, which may take months or years.

This can be avoided by establishing a foundation of clear principles that everyone buys into. Such principles must provide not just the *what* observations but also solid *why* answers that can be used to develop *how* solutions.

These work best when grown naturally out of consistent application of a shared moral value system based on belief in a higher power or influence. Communication, respect, and inclusion will allow the value system to function. When consequences are necessary, they cannot appear arbitrary, random, or made up on the fly. Rather, they must fit within the context of the foundational principles that have already been established and agreed to by family members.

Once a well-structured environment is operating within the family, it must be applied wisely and flexibly as children develop. It is true that entire families can have differing levels of maturity based on the culture created within the home.

In addition, parents cannot be afraid to adjust to new realities as circumstances change. The best way to avoid surprises from these changing dynamics is to remain focused. You cannot allow your attention to be overly diverted with work, hobbies, or other interests. This level of diligence does more than produce foundational characteristics, like kindness, among family members. It also creates an environment where parents and children can face life while standing on stable ground. Such good ground is cultivated through making solid, consistent, foundational decisions.

What are these foundational decisions? They are the fundamental choices that individuals and families need only make once in their lives and reinforce daily. Such choices make life simpler. Many have been discussed in the preceding chapters. We have included below a couple of additional examples of blended-family choices that have made systemic changes in our home.

A Calm Voice

One of our foundational choices is that we do not argue or raise our voices. This has created a calm, safe atmosphere in our family. It does not mean we always agree or that there has never been a raised voice. We are human. However, this means when we do err, there is nearly an immediate check in our behavior followed by an apology. This keeps the moment as a passing phenomenon rather than allowing it to escalate.

Another is that we do not use foul or unacceptable language anywhere, especially in the home. We have three categories of unacceptable language.

1. We do not take God's or the Lord's names in vain. This includes using the popular phrases that have become unconscious punctuation in modern conversations. The *why* is that we reverence our Creator and respect and appreciate His hand in our lives. We also do not use the popular alternative words for this because we understand that it is the meaning behind what you say and not just the words that make a statement inappropriate. Using surrogate words or terms does not change the venom or thoughtlessness of the statement.

2. We do not use swear, vulgar, or crude words or what would be considered foul language in their common forms or in their alternative variations. We refrain from providing examples here for obvious reasons.

3. We discourage the use of what we refer to as *garbage talk*. These are demeaning or mean-spirited words or phrases. Examples include hurtful words or phrases like "shut-up," "whatever," "I don't care," "suck," "I hate …" or a host of other words that lower or darken the level of conversation toward ignorance. Garbage talk also includes words that demean other peoples, races, cultures, religions, lifestyles, or a person's appearance or intelligence.

You may feel this is extreme, but it has worked well in our family. It helps maintain a level of respect and kindness that underpins our dealings with each other. It has also produced more creative and enlightened conversation. It is true that we will occasionally hear words in our home that need to be added to the *garbage talk* list. Such foundational family decisions grow naturally out of positive family communication and openness encouraged within the principles discussed.

Clark's extensive investment banking and corporate finance career taught him an important lesson on this subject. While working and negotiating with top business and government officials throughout the world there has been one principle to which he has never seen an exception. When an individual uses anger or foul language in the business, political, or social setting it always has been an indication of personal insecurity and that the person has a lack of confidence in the position being taken. It also almost always telegraphs imminent collapse or lack of authority. That's something to think about before considering the use of profanity or anger to intimidate or force a point in family or other settings. It is not an act of power; rather, it always indicates desperation, insecurity, immaturity, and weakness—not to mention a lack of creative thought and a shallow vocabulary.

Empower Your Family

The idea that a blended family has established principles of conduct based on foundational decisions to guide individual interactions is an empowering concept. Because a family makes this decision together, each member knows when faced with challenges in society away from the home that they are never truly alone. Our impression is that families and individuals either have firm principles or they are in constant daily and hourly negotiation on where to stand given each changing situation. An atmosphere of constant negotiation is a slippery slope for both adults and children because it robs them of clear decision-making, leaving only infinite shades of gray.

A family that is trying to establish proper rules in the moment or on the fly is one that has no standards. Children resent random, spur-of-the-moment, or arbitrary rules, punishment, or consequences, even if they know their behavior warrants some kind of discipline. They quickly learn that everything is negotiable or that on certain subjects the standards are not real. This can produce attempts to manipulate or dominate. It almost always leads to feelings of unfairness or persecution, which can drive wedges between family members.

We have witnessed situations where the parents have been emotionally beaten down by one or more children, allowing that child to intimidate the family. Such parents end up walking about, as if on eggshells, doing all they can to avoid conflict. The ultimate cost of allowing a child to develop destructive, abusive, and unhealthy behaviors is never worth the short-term gain of avoiding conflict. Outside counseling may be the only way to address the situation.

Blended families may face difficulty or disagreement when attempting to put a framework in place. Life may feel chaotic for a while. However, as the family perseveres, behavior will improve. If such framework is left until after the marriage or move in date, the family will be fighting an uphill battle it may be unable to win.

Clark and another individual were asked to manage a youth basketball league for a couple of years. The first year was a nightmare. The referees were volunteers who rarely showed. He and his associate ended up refereeing all eighty-two games. Bad behavior among players, coaches, and fans was a problem although there was improvement over prior years. The governing board of the league recognized the progress and asked them to do it a second year. They agreed to proceed with two conditions.

1. Each team would provide a referee for each of the team's games. The designated referees, in most cases there were three or four alternatives from each team designated, would be required to attend league provided training or they could not referee, and the team could not participate. The designated referees ended up being assistant coaches or parents.

2. A team unable to provide a trained referee for any specific game forfeited that game.

There was initial concern regarding the potential for biased refereeing and altercations. The second season proceeded with interesting results. Neither Clark nor his associate refereed a single game although they attended many games to observe. In addition, there were no discipline problems or altercations in any game with fans, players, or coaches. The board viewed it as miraculous. It was a dramatic improvement, but the miracle had a heavy dose of planning, structure, and buy in. When individuals are given responsibility and training, expectations are made clear, and rules consistently enforced, things usually work pretty well. Empowering people and teaching correct principles are the road to self-reliance.

It is the same with a blended family. As you apply the principles of success, allow personal responsibility, and live them yourself, a miraculous change will flow over your family. It will not happen all at once, and certainly there will be bumps along the way. Some family members may struggle. A few may choose not to participate for a while. But you will make progress.

You Can Do It

Make a commitment to stay engaged with each of your children. Confidence that they are not in this alone will grow. They will begin to see family members as allies who are committed to their success. Happiness and a healthy environment are irresistibly attractive.

Your home can be happier, your lives smoother, and your children unchained from the burdens they carry. They will be rendered free to become someone more than they otherwise would have been. It takes hard work, self-sacrifice, godly patience, never giving up, and a complete devotion to each other. But it is worth every moment, every effort, every tear, and every worry. If we can do it beginning from where we had to start, you can too.

It all comes down to setting the stage from the beginning. Compassion, positive attitude, a commitment to communication, achieving family goals, and having fun will win out. Do it so everyone is able to recognize they have value. It is a delicate balance that requires constant fine tuning, but it does work. Blending can be a fun adventure. For us it has been a rewarding and satisfying one. After fourteen years, we remain very much in love. Our children know and feel that love every day.

In conclusion, we will refer again to music. David Archuleta, a former *American Idol* contestant, has performed an appropriate and uplifting song written by Stephanie Mabey. It is called *Glorious*. It expresses the process through which all blended families travel:

> *It's like a symphony just keep listening,*
> *and pretty soon you'll start to figure out your part.*
> *Everyone plays a piece and there are melodies in each one of us,*
> *oh, it's glorious.*

The chorus above describes the successful process in which we all are involved—not just the creation but the beautification of a blended family. We are still learning to play this music together and individually. Of course, there are the occasional sour notes or poorly tuned strings. We also have some who are yet to pick up their instruments and add their talents to our orchestra. But we sound a lot better than we did fourteen years ago. Regardless, we keep working at it and never give up. We blend because of, and sometimes in spite of, ourselves. Yet, each individual is still allowed to solo with their own unique melody. Blending a family gives us the opportunity to witness miracles every day. *It truly is glorious.*

Acknowledgments

ttempting to put into a few chapters the magic and beauty in which we have been privileged to participate has been a Herculean task. We are grateful to our children and grandchildren for providing a life filled with examples and insights, allowing us to illustrate our principles of success. An attempt to relate all of the challenges, fun, and inspiring moments would fill volumes.

We express our sincere and thanks to Nancy and Alan Peterson, a blended family themselves, for readings, advice, and direction during this process and to Lora and Don Albrecht for details surrounding the Mount St. Helen's eruption. Special thanks to Travis and Shaunna Burbidge for insight into the realm of GPS technology and how the satellite system upon which it depends is monitored and regulated. The kind and patient guidance of Elizabeth Alley in our initial in-depth edit set us on a critical path, preparing us for our ultimate publisher review. The expert involvement of our publisher Deep River Books and their trust in our ability to adjust and deliver has made a lasting impact on the quality and focus of this effort. Thanks to Bill, Tamara, Alexis, Andy, and all our Deep River friends in the publishing process. We cannot overlook the critical and patient efforts of our editor Barbara Scott. Her support and kind direction always make the book more insightful and her own blended-family experience brought valuable perspective another editor might not have been able to contribute.

No acknowledgment would be complete without expressing our sincere gratitude to our long-time friend and go-to illustrator Karl C. Hepworth for his work on the family figures on the front cover. We also appreciate the time our favorite Aulani server, Lauren Walters, took to assist as we developed the back-cover author photograph. We wish Lauren all the best as she contemplates establishing a blended family of her own. Thanks as well to our daughter Shauntae Browning for her assistance with the back-cover photo and to Andy and his team at Deep River for the creative ideas and delivery of an amazing cover design.

Books go through several lives to make it into the hands of those they can most inspire and encourage. Our deep appreciation goes out to Robin Surface, Edge Book Printing Solutions and Fideli Publishing, Inc. for the extraordinary work and professionalism that went into the process necessary to extend the Family Blender's life through Ingram Spark. Your patience and expertise has moved us from the dark ages of publishing into the light of a beautiful dawn.

We also thank our neighbors, extended family, friends, teachers, spontaneous mentors, community, and those who have been there for us at times when we needed extra encouragement. Crossing each of your paths occurred on days when only you could make a critical difference.

Our gratitude is also extended to a loving heavenly Father who has always been there with comfort, answers to prayers, and guidance. Our path would have ended badly were it not for His divine light leading the way, especially during the darkest hours. His patient hand in our lives has taught us that no one is ever alone.

Most of all we want to thank those single parents and members of blended families who inspire us every day through their simple efforts to hold things together long enough to learn and grow. Your blogs, posts, emails, personal advice, and comments help others desperately seeking ideas to make it through the day or week. Your shared experiences allow us to step back and see our world through fresh eyes. It brings perspective and hope. There must be a special place in heaven for those who face the single- and blended-family gauntlet and never give up. We are honored to walk in your presence.

Sources

Albrecht, Donald and Lora. "Personal Experience: Mt. Saint Helen's Eruption, May 1980." Personal Phone Interview by Clark R. Burbidge, June 2017.

A Shot in the Dark. Directed by Blake Edwards. Hollywood, CA: MGM Studios, 1964. DVD.

Baum, L. Frank. *The Wonderful Wizard of Oz*, Chicago: George M. Hill Company, 1900.

Brantley, Steve, Myers, Bobby. "Mount St. Helens – From the 1980 Eruption to 2000." U.S. Geological Survey Fact Sheet, Last Modified May 2005. http://pubs.usgs.gov/fs/2000/fs036-00/.

Burbidge, Clark R. *Life on the Narrow Path: A Mountain Biker's Guide to Spiritual Growth in Troubled Times*, Springville, UT: Bonneville Books an imprint of Cedar Fort Inc., 2011.

Burbidge, Travis and Shaunna. "Observations on GPS Technology." Personal Phone Interview by Clark R. Burbidge, June 2017.

Canfield, Jack, Hansen, Mark Victor, Donnelly, Mark, Donnelly, Chrissy and De Angelis, Barbara Ph.D. *Chicken Soup for the Couple's Soul.* Deerfield, Florida: Health Communications, Inc., 1999.

Cherlin, Andrew J. *The Marriage Go-Round: The State of Marriage and the Family in America Today.* New York: First Vintage Books, Random House, 2010.

Cohn, D'Vera. "Love and Marriage." Pew Research Center: Social & Demographic Trends, February 13, 2013. http://www.pewsocialtrends.org/2013/02/13/love-and-marriage/.

Davis, Jeanie Lerche. "Family Dinners Are Important." WebMD Archive, Reviewed 2007. http://www.webmd.com/a-to-z-guides/features/family-dinners-are-important.

Frost, Robert. *The Road Not Taken: A Selection of Robert Frost's Poems.* New York: Holt Paperbacks. Revised edition 2002.

Griffin, R. Morgan. "Give Your Body a Boost—With Laughter." WebMD Archive, http://www.webmd.com/balance/features/give-your-body-boost-with-laughter.

Groundhog Day. Directed by Harold Ramis. Culver City, CA: Columbia Pictures, 1993. DVD.

Hinckley, Gordon B. *One Bright Shining Hope: Messages for Women.* Salt Lake City: Deseret Book, 2006.

Hubbard, Elbert Green, as quoted in Heartwarming Family Quotes. https://www.great-inspirational-quotes.com/family-quotes.html.

Jayson, Sharon. "Each family dinner adds up to benefits for adolescents." USA Today, March 2013. http://www.usatoday.com/story/news/nation/2013/03/24/family-dinner-adolescent-benefits/2010731.

Kelly, Grace Patricia, Interview: Family Circle Magazine as referenced and quoted by Harold B. Lee "Maintain Your Place as a Woman." *Ensign Magazine.* February 1972.

Kjellstrom, Bjorn. *Be Expert with Map & Compass: The Complete Orienteering Handbook.* New Jersey: John Wiley & Sons, Inc. 2010.

Klein, Sarah. "8 reasons to make time for family dinner." CNN Living, May 2011. http://www.cnn.com/2011/10/25/living/family-dinner-h/index.html.

Lennon, John. "Real Love." The Beatles, Apple 58544, 1996. Compact Disc.

Mary Poppins. Directed by Robert Stevenson. Burbank, CA: Walt Disney Studios, 1964. DVD.

Mabey, Stephanie. *Glorious*, ASIN: B008Y0VOA8, 2012. Amazon Download.

Mandela, Nelson. AZQuotes. http://www.azquotes.com/author/9365-Nelson_Mandela/tag/making-a-difference.

National Fatherhood Initiative. "Father Absence and Involvement Statistics." https://www.fatherhood.org/fatherhood-data-statistics.

National Stepfamily Resource Center. Last modified December 1, 2015, http://www.stepfamilies.info/stepfamily-fact-sheet.php.

References imbedded in http://www.stepfamilies.info/stepfamily-fact-sheet.php.

Bumpass, L.L., Raley, R.K., & Sweet, J.A. "The changing character of stepfamilies: Implications of cohabitation and non-marital childbearing, Demography." 32, 425-436, 1995.

Bramlett, M.D., & Mosher, W.D. *Cohabitation, marriage, divorce, and remarriage in the United States. Vital and health statistics* (Series 23, No.22). Hyattsville, MD: National Center for Health Statistics, 2002.

Cherlin, A. J. *Demographic trends in the United States: A review of the research in the 2000s. Journal of Marriage and Family. 72,* 403-419, 2010.

Kreider, R.M. *Number, timing, and duration of marriages and divorces: 2001. Current Population Reports.* Washington, DC: Government Printing Office, 2005.

Kreider, R.M. *Improvements to demographic household data in the current population survey: 2007. Current Population Reports.* Washington, DC: Government Printing Office, 2008.

Kreider, R.M. & Ellis, R. *Number, timing, and duration of marriages and divorces: 2009. Current Population Reports.* Washington, DC: Government Printing Office, 2011.

Pryor, J. (Ed.). *The international handbook of stepfamilies: Policy and practice in legal, research, and clinical environments.* Hoboken, New Jersey: John Wiley & Sons, Inc., 2008.

U.S. Bureau of the Census. *Families and living arrangements. Current Population Reports.* Washington, DC: Government Printing Office, 2008.

U.S. Bureau of the Census. *America's families and living arrangements. Current Population Reports* (Table C9). Washington DC: Government Printing Office, 2009.

Newsone. "72 Percent of Black Kids Raised by Single Parent, 25% Overall in U.S." https://newsone.com/1195075/children-single-parents-u-s-american/, 2011.

Parke, Mary. "Are Married Parents Really Better for Children?: What Research Says About the Effects of Family Structure on Child Well-Being." Center for Law and Social Policy, May 2003. http://www.clasp.org/resources-and-publications/states/0086.pdf.

Paul The Apostle. *Holy Bible: Authorized King James Version, The First Epistle of Paul The Apostle to the Corinthians,* Chapter 13, verses 3-13. Salt Lake City, Utah: Intellectual Reserve, Inc. 1979.

Pew Research Study. "The Decline of Marriage and the Rise of the New Family." Pew Research Center: Social & Demographic Trends. November 18, 2010.

Pew Research Center. "Parenting in America." Pew Research Center: Social & Demographic Trends. December 15, 2015.

Radmacher, Mary Anne, *Courage Doesn't Always Roar.* San Francisco: Conrai Press, 2009.

"Smart Stepfamilies." Last modified April 24, 2014. Imbedded reference Karney, Garvan & Thomas, Rand Corporation, 2003. http://www.smartstepfamilies.com/view/statistics.

Spiegel, Jill and Brozic, Joe. *How to Talk to Anyone About Anything: Secrets to Connecting.* 92, 94. Minneapolis: Goal Getters, 2008.

St. John. *Holy Bible: Authorized King James Version, The Gospel According to St. John,* Chapter 14, verses 15-18. Salt Lake City, Utah: Intellectual Reserve, Inc. 1979.

St. Mark. *Holy Bible: Authorized King James Version, The Gospel According to St. Mark,* Chapter 6, versus 32-44. Salt Lake City, Utah: Intellectual Reserve, Inc. 1979.

Sweeney, M. M. "Remarriage and stepfamilies: Strategic sites for family scholarship in the 21st century." *Journal of Marriage and Family.* 72, 667-684, 2010.

Thaik, Dr. Cynthia. "Why Laughter is Good for Your Health." *Huffington Post*, March 16, 2014, http://www.huffingtonpost.com/dr-cynthia-thaik/laughing-health_b_4519611.html.

The Stepfamily Foundation. Stepfamily Statistics, (Copyright 2021) https://www.stepfamily.org/stepfamily-statistics.html

UP. Directed by Pete Docter. Burbank, CA: Walt Disney Studios, 2009. DVD.

U.S. Bureau of the Census. "Families and living arrangements. Current Population Reports," Washington, DC: Government Printing Office, 2004.

U.S. Bureau of the Census. "Families and living arrangements. Current Population Reports," Washington, DC: Government Printing Office, 2005.

U.S. Bureau of the Census. "Families and living arrangements. Current Population Reports," Washington, DC: Government Printing Office, 2022.

Wallace, Catherine M. "Goodreads-Quotable Quotes." https://www.goodreads.com/quotes/241128-listen-earnestly-to-anything-your-children-want-to-tell-you.

Winfrey, Oprah. "The Quotations Page: Quotations by Author." http://www.quotationspage.com/quotes/Oprah_Winfrey (Attributed to a statement in O Magazine).